STUDENT UNIT

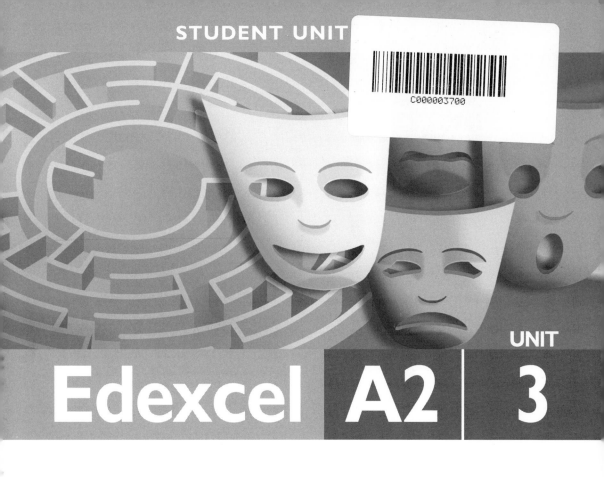

Edexcel A2 | UNIT 3

Psychology

Criminological and Child Psychology

Christine Brain

Philip Allan Updates, an imprint of Hodder Education, an Hachette UK company, Market Place, Deddington, Oxfordshire OX15 0SE

Orders
Bookpoint Ltd, 130 Milton Park, Abingdon, Oxfordshire OX14 4SB
tel: 01235 827827
fax: 01235 400401
e-mail: education@bookpoint.co.uk

Lines are open 9.00 a.m.–5.00 p.m., Monday to Saturday, with a 24-hour message answering service. You can also order through the Philip Allan Updates website: www.philipallan.co.uk

ISBN 978-0-340-94879-8

First printed 2009
Impression number 5 4 3 2
Year 2014 2013 2012 2011 2010

This guide has been written specifically to support students preparing for the Edexcel A2 Psychology Unit 3 examination. The content has been neither approved nor endorsed by Edexcel and remains the sole responsibility of the author.

Typeset by Phoenix Photosetting, Chatham, Kent
Printed by MPG Books, Bodmin

Hachette UK's policy is to use papers that are natural, renewable and recyclable products and made from wood grown in sustainable forests. The logging and manufacturing processes are expected to conform to the environmental regulations of the country of origin.

Contents

Introduction

Content Guidance

Criminological psychology

Child psychology

Questions and Answers

Criminological psychology

Child psychology

Introduction

About this guide

This is a guide to two applications within Unit 3 of the Edexcel A2 specification: Criminological Psychology and Child Psychology.

This guide:
- is not a textbook — there is no substitute for reading the required material and taking notes
- does not tell you the actual questions on your paper, or give you the answers!

Aims of the guide

The aim of this guide is to provide you with a clear understanding of the requirements of Unit 3 of the A2 specification — focusing on two applications, as necessary for the unit — and to advise you on how best to meet these requirements.

This guide will look at:
- the psychology you need to know about
- what you need to be able to do and what skills you need
- how you could go about learning the necessary material
- what is being examined
- what you should expect in the examination for this application
- how you could tackle the different styles of exam question
- the format of the exam, including what questions might look like
- how questions are marked, including examples of answers, with examiner's comments

How to use this guide

A good way to use this guide is to read it through in the order in which it is presented. Alternatively, you can consider each topic in the Content Guidance section, and then turn to the relevant question in the Questions and Answers section. Whichever way you use the guide, try some of the questions yourself to test your learning. You should know enough about the marking by this time to try to grade your own answers. If you are working with someone else, mark each other's answers.

The more you work on what is needed, the better. Have other textbooks available too — you will need access to all the relevant information.

Learning and revision strategies

This section gives suggestions for effective learning and revision.

How to learn the material

- Make notes, be concise and use your own notes for final revision.
- Have a separate sheet of paper for each application.
- For each application, note down the five headings (definitions, methodology, content, studies in detail and key issue/practical) and use them as a guide. Leave room to fit your notes in under each heading.
- Read through each section, then make notes as needed (very briefly).
- Be sure to make notes on evaluation points.
- Finally, note down briefly three things about a key issue that describe the issue, and six 'facts' linking concepts to the issue.

Another useful method is to use cards for each topic. Have the topic heading on one side of the card and brief notes on the other. Remember to note down equal amounts of knowledge and evaluation.

Revision plan

- Start at least 4 weeks before the exam date (sooner if possible).
- Using times that suit you (6 a.m. might be a great time to study!), draw up a blank timetable for each of the weeks.
- On the timetable, fill in all your urgent commitments (cancel as many plans as you can).
- Divide up what is left, allocating slots to all your subjects as appropriate. Don't forget to build in meal times, breaks and time for sleep.
- Stick to the plan if at all possible, but if you have to, amend it as you go.
- When studying, have frequent, short rests and no distractions.

Examination structure and skills

Unit 3 consists of four applications of psychology: criminological, child, health and sport psychology. You must select *two* of these applications to study and you will have to answer questions on both of them in the exam. This guide looks at two of them — criminological and child psychology.

There will be one whole question for each application, which will be divided into separate parts. Each application covers five areas: definitions, methodology, content, studies in detail and key issue/practical. There will not be a question for each area of the application — questions for each application will range across these five areas.

Questions and assessment objectives

Each of the two A2 exam papers (Units 3 and 4) has some short-answer questions, some extended-writing questions and finally extended writing (essay question) at the end.

The assessment objectives (AOs) of the A2 exam papers are the same as for the AS papers. Briefly, they are as follows:
- AO1 — testing knowledge with understanding and good communication skills
- AO2 — testing evaluation, assessment and applications
- AO3 — testing understanding and evaluation of methodology, including other people's studies

Don't think that someone sets each paper with past papers in front of them, avoiding what has been asked before. Imagine someone trying to set an interesting paper, covering a range of topics from the five areas for each application, and balancing AO1, AO2 and AO3 marks according to the required percentages of each. It is not possible to guess what is going to be on the paper — don't try. Prepare answers for all possible questions.

Tips in this guide include words such as 'usually'. Each paper will be different, and you have to be prepared to answer whatever questions appear. For example, there are many ways that short-answer questions can be written, such as:
- 'Explain what is meant by...'
- 'Describe the procedure of...'
- 'Outline the theory...'
- 'Outline two weaknesses of...'
- 'What is the hypothesis in the study...?'

Read the question carefully and do what is asked, and you will do well.

The Unit 3 exam

Unit 3 is assessed in a 90-minute exam. Answers are written in a booklet similar to those used at GCSE. There are 60 marks available. This means you need to score around 1 mark per minute, with 30 minutes to spare for reading and thinking. In general, you can expect to gain 1 mark for each point that answers the question, or for elaboration of a point. Answers must be communicated 'clearly and effectively' (this is part of AO1). Avoid one-word answers unless they are asked for. The final essay question is expected to be worth 12 marks.

Overall, marks are awarded as follows:
- About 30% of the marks (around 18 marks when considering both applications) are awarded for knowledge and understanding (AO1).
- About 40% (around 24 marks when considering both applications) are for evaluation and comment and application to unfamiliar situations (AO2).
- About 30% (around 18 marks when considering both applications) are for knowledge and assessment of practical work, both your own and other people's.

In practice you can simply focus on revising equal amounts of AO1, AO2 and AO3 (knowledge, evaluation and practical work) and answer each question as it arises.

Two types of marking

There are two types of marking. One type is point-based marking, where 1 mark is awarded per point made, and there are also marks for elaboration of a point. The other type of marking involves 'levels', which means there are bands of marks that are awarded according to the quality of the answer. An example is the following mark scheme for a question asking for the IV for a study for 2 marks:

- 0 marks — no appropriate material (e.g. giving the DV)
- 1 mark — not fully operationalised (e.g. giving one side of the IV)
- 2 marks — fully operationalised, giving both or all sides of the IV, and possibly an example

Questions about your own practicals are marked according to levels and quality — for example, if you are asked about planning your content analysis a thorough answer will get full marks and a very weak answer will get very few marks.

The essays are also marked using levels and according to quality. For example, if you are asked about two explanations for criminal or antisocial behaviour and you only discuss one explanation you will be in the middle band somewhere. It is in the levels marking that your writing skills are assessed, including how well you select material for your answer, and the quality of your spelling, grammar and use of terminology.

Table 1 shows some examples of how AO1 injunctions are used and Table 2 shows examples of AO2 injunctions. Table 3 shows some examples of AO3 questions, which can include various kinds of injunctions but must be about practicals and methodology in some way. Note that it is not so much the word itself (e.g. 'describe') as the whole question that makes it AO1, AO2 or AO3. The figures in brackets suggest the mark allocation you might expect for such a question.

Table 1 Examples of AO1 questions/injunctions

Type of question	What is being asked for
Describe a theory... (5)	Say what something is (a theory in this case). Imagine describing the theory to someone who knows little about the subject.
Identify a theory... (1)	Give enough information so that the examiner can understand what is being referred to. For example, if asked to identify an 'attachments' theory, the answer might be 'Bowlby's maternal deprivation hypothesis'.
Identify a study... (1)	Name either the study or the psychologist(s). For example, if the question asks for a study, the answer might be 'Loftus and Palmer' or 'the "smashed glass" study'.
Outline a definition of the ... application (3)	Follow the instructions for 'describe', but remember that this injunction requires less detail, and hence carries fewer marks.
Describe Curtiss's study of Genie... (5)	Try to give the aim of the study, the procedure/case background, the results/case analysis and the conclusion(s). (Note the difference here between studies and case studies — 'Genie' is a case study.)

Table 2 Examples of AO2 questions/injunctions

Type of question	What is being asked for
Outline a strength of... (2)	You are asked to outline something, so the injunction seems to be AO1 (i.e. knowledge and understanding). However, as what must be outlined is a strength (in this case), meaning that you have to *evaluate* something, this question carries AO2 marks.
With regard to the stimulus material above, explain... (6)	You are asked to refer to some stimulus material and apply your knowledge of psychology to explain the material in some way. Refer to the material at least once in your answer.
Compare two explanations for criminal behaviour... (6)	You are asked to choose two explanations for criminal behaviour and then write about how they are similar and/or how they are different. 'And/or' means you can do both or one or the other.
Assess how far an evolution theory of attachments is a useful theory... (4)	You can consider practical uses of the theory of attachments, or you can evaluate the theory itself, because that would shed light on how useful it might be — but focus on its usefulness.

Table 3 Examples of AO3 questions/injunctions

Type of question	What is being asked for
Outline the aim(s) of your article/content analysis... (2)	You are asked to say what the purpose of your study was, that is, to briefly state what you were trying to find out. 'Outline' sounds like an AO1 injunction, but as this is about your practical, it is an AO3 question.
Evaluate one of these studies — either Yuille and Cutshall (1986), Charlton et al. (2000) or Gesch et al. (2003). (5)	You will have covered one of these studies but probably not all of them. Choose the one you know and give comments, criticisms, good points and so on. Consider strengths and weaknesses of the research method, perhaps, or make criticisms of the ethics involved. Look at alternative findings or consider whether justified conclusions are drawn. Although 'evaluate' sounds like an AO2 injunction, the question is about someone else's study, which is psychology in practice, so it is an AO3 question. Yuille and Cutshall (1986) is explained in this guide.

Conclusions: use of injunctions and the AO1/AO2/AO3 split

Don't just think of a word in the question as being the whole question. For example, you might think 'describe' is an AO1 command because it seems to ask for knowledge. However, 'describe a strength...' is an AO2 injunction because it asks for evaluation; and 'describe the procedure of your practical' is an AO3 question because it asks about psychology in practice. 'Discuss' could signal AO2 marks if you are asked to 'discuss the usefulness of...': because you are considering how useful something is, you are doing more than showing knowledge about it. The best approach is to *answer the question*. If you pay attention to the question and understand it, all should be well.

introduction

The specification gives a list of what injunction words mean in your course so you could look at that to check your understanding. However, the question should indicate clearly what you have to do. Remember that the specification, sample papers and sample mark scheme are on the Edexcel website (**www.edexcel.com**).

Essentially, then, you have to learn material so you know and understand it, and then plan some criticisms, comments and evaluation points. As a rule of thumb, be sure to learn or plan as many evaluation and comment points as you learn information points.

Differences between AS and A2

Although a lot of what is true for AS still applies to A2 — for example, the AO1, AO2 and AO3 assessment objectives — the A2 exams require higher-level skills.

At A2, more marks are given for AO2 (evaluation and comment) than for AO1 (knowledge and understanding). This is different from what is required at AS. It means you need to comment, evaluate, assess, consider strengths, and so on, more than you need to give information. When you are making notes and preparing answers to exam questions, remember to concentrate on criticisms. Whenever you read an evaluation point, note it down and learn it.

Greater depth is also required in your answers at A2. For example, you could be asked about two ways that one developmental issue might affect a child's development. The specification does not say that you need studies and evidence, but they could be useful. Remember to refer to the assessment objectives outlined in this introduction. The specification might not ask you specifically to learn studies of child-rearing styles in different cultures (though you are asked to describe and evaluate cross-cultural issues regarding child-rearing styles), but you will need to refer to relevant evidence to support your answers (AO2). Psychology is built on evidence from studies, so when revising it is useful to have a list of names of studies and a brief outline of what each is about. Note also that Unit 3 is about applications of psychology, so be ready to apply your knowledge.

Content
Guidance

This section provides an overview of what you need to learn for the Criminological Psychology and Child Psychology applications of Unit 3. Each application is divided into the following areas:

- Definition of the application
- Methodology/how science works
- Content
- Studies in detail
- Evidence in practice: key issue and practical

Note that choices are made for you in this guide, in order to limit the material. However, if you have studied a different choice it is probably better to revise that, rather than learn something new at this stage.

Note also that when studying your two applications you must include one analysis of articles and one content analysis. In this guide the Criminological Psychology application has the article analysis and the Child Psychology application has the content analysis.

Criminological psychology

Definition of the application

This section looks at what criminological psychology is about and at some of the key terms.

Criminological psychology is about crime and antisocial behaviour.

- **Crime** (a key term) is defined as an act against the law and implies a punishment or treatment to avoid someone re-offending. For example, stealing, murder and fraud are crimes that are against the law and carry with them a punishment. They are against social norms too. Crime is said to be **socially constructed** because it represents what a particular culture thinks is wrong, and so what is considered a crime differs across societies.

- **Recidivism** (a key term) involves someone repeating a crime or behaviour for which they have been punished or treated (that is, returning to their criminal activities). For example, if someone convicted of burglary and punished is freed after the appropriate length of time and then steals again, this will increase recidivism figures.

- **Antisocial behaviour** (a key term) is behaviour that is not necessarily against the law but that the majority of people do not like and do not approve of. It is behaviour that affects people negatively; the term is often used for aggressive behaviour. Antisocial behaviour can turn into or can be crime. Recently in the UK, ASBOs (antisocial behaviour orders) have been created to prevent such behaviour.

- **Criminological psychology** looks at explanations and causes of crime, features of crime and antisocial behaviour, and also treatments for crime and antisocial behaviour. Forensic psychologists (as 'criminal psychologists' are usually termed) are also concerned with identifying criminals, the processes involved in court procedures, and rehabilitation (to avoid recidivism).

> **Tip**
>
> A good way to extend a definition when there are 3 marks available is to add an example.

Other key terms you might be asked about are defined in this content section as they arise: modelling (page 19), stereotyping (page 26), eyewitness memory (page 29) and token economy (page 35).

Methodology/how science works

This section looks at laboratory and field experiments, giving description and evaluation.

Laboratory experiments

Laboratory experiments can be described as:

- having an **independent variable (IV)** manipulated by the researcher and a **dependent variable (DV)** measured to observe the changes brought about by the IV manipulation
- following scientific method, where a **hypothesis** is derived from a theory, there is testing of some sort and then the hypothesis is accepted or rejected
- taking place in a controlled and artificial environment
- involving careful **controls** of **extraneous variables**, such as **participant variables** (things about the participants, such as hunger and age) and **situational variables** (things about the situation, such as noise and time of day)
- having careful controls so that cause-and-effect conclusions can be drawn (because, if only the IV is changed, only the IV can cause change in the DV)

For example, Loftus and Palmer (1974) showed that changing a verb in a question from 'hit' to 'smashed' (or another verb) can change the estimate of the speed of a car.

Tip

Note that an example can help a description but you should only give one (such as Loftus and Palmer (1974) in this case), as there is only likely to be 1 mark available for an example.

Laboratory experiments used to assess witness effectiveness

When applying psychology to the real world, for example to court proceedings, it is important that the information is solid and evidence-based. Laboratory experiments are as scientific and sound as it is possible to be in psychology. From them cause-and-effect conclusions can be drawn: if a psychologist can show, using laboratory experimental method, that leading questions give biased answers, for example, then the police and others can believe them. Elizabeth Loftus (with others) undertook many laboratory experiments to show that witnesses were not as effective as might be thought.

Loftus followed a basic method; the following points give brief information about some of her experiments.

- She gathered students to be participants, showed them a film and asked them questions about what they had seen.
- One example is Loftus and Palmer (1974), who showed that changing a verb in a question from 'hit' to 'smashed' (or another verb) can change the estimate of the speed of a car.
- In another study (Loftus and Zanni 1975) the researchers asked either 'Did you see the broken headlight?' or 'Did you see a broken headlight?' to determine whether the use of 'the' or 'a' affected the witnesses' accounts. It was found that the participants were more likely to say they saw a broken headlight (although there was none) if they were asked using 'the' than if asked using 'a'.

- In another study Loftus (1975) asked (after the participants had seen a film of a car accident) 'How fast was the car going when it passed the barn?'. Later she asked participants whether they saw a barn or not (there was in fact no barn): 2.7% of the control group who were not asked how fast the car was going when it passed the barn said they saw a barn, compared with 17.3% of the participants who were asked the question about the speed of the car past the barn.

These three studies (which look at the effects of changing the verb in a question, changing 'a' to 'the' in a question, and asking about a non-existent barn) all show that witnesses are not very effective and eyewitness testimony is unreliable. Loftus was testing **eyewitness memory**, which involves how witnesses remember an event, and she thought that memory was not like a tape recorder but reconstructive, as Bartlett proposed, and that people use **schemas**. Therefore memory is unreliable. Such issues are returned to later. As Loftus used laboratory experiments, her findings were said to be scientific, reliable, objective and credible.

Laboratory features of Loftus and Palmer (1974)
- The IV was the change of verb and the DV was the estimate of speed in miles per hour.
- The hypothesis was that participants who were given a question with a 'stronger' verb (e.g. 'smashed' is stronger than 'hit') would give a higher estimate of speed than those with a less strong verb.
- This is a one-tailed hypothesis in that the 'stronger' the verb the higher the estimate of speed is predicted to be.
- All participants watched the same filmed information, as a control.
- All participants were asked the same questions except for the change in verb, as a control.
- The study was carried out in artificial controlled conditions.
- The procedure is well documented so that the study is replicable.

Evaluation of laboratory experiments
Laboratory experiments can be evaluated by looking at **reliability**, **objectivity**, **credibility**, **validity** and **generalisability**. In general they are said to be good with regard to all but validity. The following table summarises their strengths and weaknesses.

Strengths and weaknesses of laboratory experiments

Strengths	Weaknesses
• Laboratory experiments are replicable because of strong controls, so they are testable for reliability	• Laboratory experiments are not ecologically valid, because they do not take place in the participant's natural setting
• Laboratory experiments use scientific methodology, such as forming a hypothesis from a theory and controlling all aspects except the IV	• Laboratory experiments might not be valid with regard to the task — for example, watching a car accident on film is not the same as watching it in real life

Tip
Loftus and Palmer's (1974) study is described and evaluated on page 30.

The usefulness of laboratory experiments in criminological psychology
Strengths
- Laboratory experiments are scientific: they allow cause-and-effect conclusions to be drawn and the objectivity implies firm conclusions.
- The careful design to control variables means that a study can be repeated and so the findings tend to be reliable.
- Courts look for proof from the police, and witness testimony needs to be accurate if someone is to be convicted on the basis of it, so strong evidence from laboratory experiments is needed. Laboratory studies tend to be objective and reliable.

Weaknesses
- Laboratory experiments take place in a controlled artificial setting so are said to lack **ecological validity**.
- In respect of court practices, if findings are to be of use they need to be valid and about real life. As laboratory experiments involve artificial situations, such as participants watching films, they are likely to be not valid with regard to the task.
- If findings of a study are not valid or about real life they may not be generalisable. For example, asking students, as Loftus and Palmer (1974) did, might mean that findings are not generalisable to everyone of all ages, in all situations.

Reliability, validity and ethics with regard to laboratory experiments
- Laboratory experiments tend to have reliable findings because they are scientifically set up and replicable.
- They tend to have good ethics up to a point, because participants can be given the right to withdraw throughout and to an extent informed consent can be obtained, as the participants are recruited before the study and can be prepared as necessary. However, it is possible to criticise the ethics of individual laboratory experiments, for example because there is often a need for deception.
- Laboratory experiments tend to lack validity, because the setting is artificial and the task is often limited rather than resembling real life.

Field experiments

Field experiments can be described as:
- having an independent variable (IV) manipulated by the researcher and a dependent variable (DV) measured to observe the changes brought about by the IV manipulation
- following scientific method, where a hypothesis is derived from a theory, there is testing of some sort and then the hypothesis is accepted or rejected, which supports the theory or does not
- taking place in the participant's natural setting in some way — in 'the field'
- involving careful controls of extraneous variables, such as participant variables (things about the participants, such as hunger and age) and situational

variables (things about the situation, such as noise and time of day), in so far as is possible
- having careful controls so that cause-and-effect conclusions can be drawn (because, if only the IV is changed, only the IV can cause change in the DV)

For example, Maass and Köhnken (1989) found that students approached by a woman holding a syringe did less well in identifying her in a line-up later than those approached by the same woman when she was holding a pen.

Tip

Concerning the points given above, the only difference from laboratory experiments is that field experiments take place in a natural setting and so controls might not be possible to the same extent.

Field experiments used to assess witness effectiveness

Field experiments are used to assess witness effectiveness because they have the controls and scientific value of laboratory experiments and yet are more valid because they take place in a natural setting.
- Field experiments which look at witness reliability tend to follow a pattern, generally involving a researcher going up to someone (who then becomes the participant) in the street. The researcher then asks the participant something or demonstrates a characteristic. Afterwards another researcher stops the participant and asks them questions about the researcher who stopped them.
- For example, Maass and Köhnken (1989) asked 86 students who were not studying psychology to take part in their study. In their own environment (in the field) each student was approached by a woman holding either a pen or a syringe. Sometimes she said she would give them an injection; sometimes she did not. Students then had to try to pick the woman out of a line-up and those in the 'syringe' condition performed less well than those in the 'pen' condition.
- Yarmey (2004) carried out a study with a number of different conditions. A woman approached a participant in a public place and spoke to them. This study is described and evaluated later (page 33).

Field experiment features of Maass and Köhnken (1989)
- The IV is whether the woman has a pen or a syringe. Another IV is whether she says she will inject the participant or not. The DV is whether they identified the woman in a line-up or not.
- The hypothesis is that the participants will identify the woman in a line-up less often if she is holding a syringe than if she is holding a pen.
- This is a one-tailed hypothesis, because it is thought that the participants will not be able to identify the woman who approached them if their attention is focused on the syringe but they will identify the woman when she is holding the pen.
- The study is in the natural environment of the participants.

Evaluation of field experiments

The following table summarises the strengths and weaknesses of field experiments.

Strengths and weaknesses of field experiments

Strengths	Weaknesses
• Field experiments are replicable to an extent because of strong controls, so they are testable for reliability • Field experiments are ecologically valid, because they take place in the participant's natural setting	• Field experiments might not allow enough control over variables to be reliable, because the setting is not controlled the same way that it is in a laboratory experiment • Field experiments might not be valid with regard to the task either — for example, a line-up that has been set up is not the same as trying to identify a real-life criminal

The usefulness of field experiments in criminological psychology

Strengths

- Field experiments are scientific: they allow cause-and-effect conclusions to be drawn and the objectivity implies firm conclusions.
- The careful design to control variables means that a study can be repeated and so the findings tend to be reliable. An IV is manipulated and a DV measured after as many extraneous variables as possible have been controlled.
- Courts look for proof from the police, and witness testimony needs to be accurate if someone is to be convicted on the basis of it, so strong evidence from field experiments is needed. Field experiments tend to be objective and reliable and also take place in a natural setting so there is some validity.
- It is possible that field experiments are more useful than laboratory experiments with regard to applying their findings to court and police procedures, because laboratory experiments tend to lack validity (they take place in a controlled artificial setting) whereas field experiments are more valid (they take place 'in the field').

Weaknesses

- Field experiments take place in a controlled setting up to a point, because any extraneous variables that can be controlled are controlled. However, in 'the field' there are likely to be variables that cannot be controlled, such as the weather or people's experiences of the setting.
- Participants for field experiments are often people who happen to be there on the day. So the sampling is 'volunteer' to an extent and generalising might be limited because of bias in the sample.
- Field experiments use specific procedures (such as asking a participant to pick out of a line-up someone who has approached them once to ask a simple question), whereas real incidents may be more complex and/or have other features. Therefore findings might not be generalisable (for example to other witness situations), and it might not be appropriate to apply such findings to court proceedings and police procedures.

Reliability, validity and ethics with regard to field experiments
- Field experiments can be reliable because the scientific procedures tend to mean they are replicable. However, the lack of controls over certain circumstances, because the study is in a natural setting, means that replication of studies might not be exact.
- Field experiments can also be ethical because, as with laboratory studies, it is known beforehand what the procedures will be so participants can be asked for consent. However, if the setting is to be natural it often means that the participants are not informed beforehand that they are taking part.
- Field experiments tend to have validity in the sense that they take part in a natural setting. This means they have ecological validity. However, the task is still artificial as the IV is manipulated, so there might be a lack of validity to that extent.

Be ready to use the methodology material about the two experimental methods (field and laboratory) for questions asking you to compare the two methods or to link them to specific issues in criminological psychology.

Content

This section covers two explanations for criminal behaviour, three studies that look into eyewitness testimony and two ways of treating offenders.

Two explanations for criminal behaviour

This section looks first at how social learning theory explains criminal and/or antisocial behaviour and then at how such behaviour might be explained through labelling and the self-fulfilling prophecy.

If you have studied personality and how it explains criminal and/or antisocial behaviour, you could use that as one of the two explanations, along with social learning theory.

Social learning theory, role models and crime
Observational learning suggests that people imitate behaviour they have seen, and, furthermore, they tend to imitate people like them or people they look up to. Role models are observed, their behaviour is attended to and retained, and then, if there is motivation, it is reproduced. **Modelling** (a key term) refers to the reproduction of the behaviour, and it is also the term for the whole process of observing, attending, retaining, being motivated to perform the behaviour and reproducing it.

Evidence for social learning theory comes from laboratory experiments such as Bandura, Ross and Ross (1961).

A
R
R
M

You will have studied Bandura, Ross and Ross (1961) as part of your AS studies, so revise it for use here as evidence for social learning theory. It is not really about crime, but it is about antisocial behaviour (aggression), so it fits.

Social learning theory incorporates operant conditioning principles. These are that behaviour that is positively reinforced (by giving a reward) is repeated, and behaviour that is negatively reinforced (by removing something unpleasant) is also repeated. Behaviour that is punished is less likely to be repeated but punishment can be rewarding if it is the only attention given.

Aggression can be defined as actions or intentions to harm or gain advantage over someone else. These actions or intentions might not involve physical harm. Violence, on the other hand, does involve physical harm. Criminal violence is when the violent actions are against the law. Aggression can lead to violence, so controlling aggression can mean controlling violence, and thus controlling crime.

Lozza & Lozza famhaus

Evaluation of social learning theory as an explanation for criminal behaviour

Tip

In evaluation give only one other explanation as there tends to be only 1 mark for an alternative explanation.

Strengths and weaknesses of social learning theory as an explanation of crime

Bandura Ross & Ross

Strengths	Weaknesses
• There is a lot of experimental evidence to show that behaviour is imitated, including evidence that demonstrates that aggressive behaviour is imitated (some of this evidence is explained in the next section when looking at the role of the media) • The theory has a practical application and can help to rehabilitate offenders, as appropriate role models can be used to help learn appropriate behaviour, alongside appropriate reinforcements	• The theory does not look at individual differences, only at how an individual is influenced by social factors; therefore, biological aspects are not considered • The theory does not account for criminal behaviour that is opportunistic and has not been observed first — it tends to account more for stealing, aggression and other crimes that are reasonably easily observed in society, rather than murders; therefore, the theory does not account for all crime • Freud's ideas would suggest that watching violence can lead to less aggressive behaviour, as it might result in catharsis and a release of aggression • A relationship between aggression in the media and aggressive acts is probably not straightforward — it is likely that other factors, such as whether aggression is modelled in the family, are important too

The role of the media in aggressive behaviour and/or crime

There is a lot of interest in whether the media have any effect on antisocial behaviour. Sadly, cases are documented where some film, programme or video game is said to have been imitated, leading to 'killing sprees', usually by young males. One example often cited is Columbine High School (1999). The question is whether violence in the media is responsible for antisocial behaviour or crimes, through social learning and operant conditioning principles.

> **Tip**
>
> In answers about the role of the media in antisocial behaviour, make sure any example you use is documented and published. For example, the children who killed the young child James Bulger were not found to have copied behaviour from a film although it was widely said that they did so. Use only evidence that is accepted, such as the Columbine High example and quite a few others. You could look some up.

Films that have been linked to violent crime include *Clockwork Orange*, *Child's Play* and *Natural Born Killers*, but it should not be thought that a direct link has been proved. Some think that there is enough evidence of a link between television violence and real-life aggression for programmes showing violence to be banned (Newson 1994). However, others think that a more in-depth analysis is needed, as any link between television programmes and real crime is likely to be focused on, in newspapers for example, and therefore sensationalised (Cumberbatch 1994).

Desensitisation and disinhibition

Two explanations of how the watching of violence on television might lead to violent actions include desensitisation and disinhibition. It is said that we can become **desensitised** to violence, which means we can get used to it, and initial feelings of shock are unlikely to be maintained, so we come to feel less strongly about it. **Disinhibition** refers to the possibility that watching actions that are far outside social norms, such as violent actions, might help to reduce our inhibitions and might lead us to do things we would not otherwise do.

> **Evaluation**
>
> – Studies testing desensitisation have to use mild violence as it would be unethical to expose participants to too much violence to see if they get used to it and therefore carry out more aggressive acts than they usually would. This means that studies lack validity to an extent, as they only focus on mild aggression and violence.

Evidence of a media link to aggression and crime

Bandura's work in developing social learning theory has led to many claims that violence in the media does cause antisocial and criminal behaviour. Many laboratory experiments back up Bandura's claims and provide evidence to support the idea of a media role in crime. As well as laboratory studies, there are field studies, such as Huesmann and Eron (1986), which used questionnaires and a longitudinal approach. Such evidence seems to show that violence on television would lead to violent behaviour.

Tip

When making a statement (such as the one above) that there is a lot of evidence for something, always back your claim up by noting some of the evidence.

Some studies involve experiments in which one group of children is shown violent television and another group acts as a control. The researchers then determine if those who watched the violence show more aggression afterwards. This method is similar to Bandura's initial research where children watched adults performing violent acts. Some other studies also involve carrying out experiments, but in the field rather than in a laboratory. Other studies use questionnaires or interviews.

Anderson and Dill (2000): a laboratory experiment

A study by Anderson and Dill (2000) looked at links between video game playing and aggression. They found that boys 'punished' another boy more if they had played a violent video game beforehand than if they had not. This was a laboratory experiment and is interesting because it is a newer study which also found a link between violence and aggressive behaviour, and also because it used violent video games rather than television.

Evaluation of Anderson and Dill (2000)

Strengths	Weaknesses
• Part of the study was a laboratory experiment with the environment controlled and an IV and a DV, so results were scientifically gathered • The experiment is replicable and can be tested for reliability, which helps to build a scientific body of knowledge • Using two different research methods gave more reliability, as the same connection was found in two different ways	• It has been claimed that Anderson and Dill's experimental study used measures of aggression that had not been **standardised** and also did not find significant results in all their measures, only in one of them; the measures of aggression were artificial both in the experiment and the survey • As it was a laboratory experiment, there was a lack of validity and the participants may have guessed the purpose of the study, so results might not reflect real life • Anderson and Dill's experiment looked at aggression immediately after playing the video games and was not able to determine if any aggressive response from playing a violent video game would last longer than a very short time

Parke et al. (1977): a field experiment

Parke et al. (1977) did a controlled study with boys in an institution for juvenile offenders. They controlled what television programmes the boys watched. Some watched programmes that included violence, whereas others watched programmes without violence. The researchers wanted to see whether watching programmes with violence made those boys carry out more aggressive acts. Not only did those who watched violence engage in more violent acts, but also those who watched non-violent programmes were in fact less aggressive than usual. It seemed that watching non-violent programmes might have had a calming effect.

> ### Evaluation
>
> + This field experiment had good controls and was carried out carefully. A cause-and-effect relationship was claimed.
> + There was the additional advantage that the study was carried out in the boys' natural setting, giving ecological validity.
> + Care was taken to give half the boys non-violent programmes to watch, so there was a control group.
> − There might be some ethical considerations, in that the boys' situation was made use of, as they had no real right to withdraw, and those who watched violence on television could be said to have been made more violent as a result.
> − Leyens et al. (1982) did a similar study and noted that the television watching and resultant aggression were singled-out factors, whereas in reality there are many influences on behaviour, not just what television programmes are watched. This is a disadvantage of controlled studies.

Singer and Singer (1981): questionnaire

Singer and Singer (1981) issued a questionnaire to parents to find out how much television their children watched. The researchers then observed the children at school to look for a relationship between television viewing and behaviour. It was found that those who watched the most television were the most aggressive. This suggests that there is a relationship between television watching and behaviour, as well as that television watching leads specifically to aggression.

> ### Evaluation
>
> − It would make a difference whether the programmes watched involved violence or not, and yet the variable was just how much television was watched. It is likely that the cause of aggressive behaviour at school is more complex than that.
> − Although it is possible to time how much television a child watches, it is unlikely that the parents had a very accurate knowledge of this.
> − Categorising aggressive behaviour, for example in the playground, is not easy and may not be a reliable or valid measure.

Sheehan (1983): correlational field study

Sheehan (1983) studied children aged 5 to 10 years old and looked for a correlation between what the children watched on television and whether they showed aggressive behaviour. Peers rated each child according to how likely they were to engage in acts causing physical harm, and this gave a measure of aggression. Sheehan also asked about the children's aggressive fantasies and gathered information about parents. It was found that there was a correlation between watching violence on television and being aggressive, and that the correlation was stronger for boys than for girls. Other factors, such as child-rearing style (e.g. if the parents rejected the child or if punishment was used) and family income, were also found to be important. Therefore, it is unlikely that there is a straightforward relationship between watching violent television programmes and behaving aggressively.

Evaluation

+ Field studies, such as this one, have validity.
+ Field studies can also have some of the advantages of laboratory experiments, in that there can be some control of variables, such as the way the dependent variable 'aggression' is measured by peer ratings in this case.
− Sheehan's is a correlational study and so does not uncover a cause-and-effect relationship. Although watching violence on television did seem to relate to violent behaviour, particularly in boys, other factors, such as parental style, were also important.
− In general, field studies do not have the same controls as laboratory experiments, and conclusions must take this into account, so they are less certain.
− Such studies look at short-term effects rather than the long-term effects of watching violence on television when young.

Huesmann and Eron (1986): correlational longitudinal study

Huesmann and Eron (1986) did a longitudinal study following people's viewing habits over 22 years and found that the more violence people watched on television, the more likely they were to have committed a criminal act by the age of 30.

Evaluation

+ Longitudinal studies are useful as they follow the same participants at different stages in their development. This means that any individual differences are controlled for, unlike in cross-sectional studies.
− This longitudinal study showed a relationship between television viewing and later violence, but factors other than what was watched on television would also have an effect.
− We cannot discount the idea that those who watch violence on television are disposed to violence in the first place. It may not be that watching violence on television leads to aggressive behaviour, but that aggressive tendencies lead to the viewing of violence.
− A problem with longitudinal studies is that so many factors are involved in development that it is hard to pinpoint one (e.g. the effect of watching television violence) and find its effect later.
− Another difficulty is that participants are likely to move or might refuse to take part at some stage. This means that the sample size is likely to be reduced considerably from the start of the study to the end, and bias can occur because of this.

Black and Bevan (1992): questionnaire

Black and Bevan (1992) asked people going to watch a film to complete two questionnaires: one before they watched the film and one afterwards. Those going to watch a film with violence tended to be more aggressive in the first place, and they were even more aggressive after watching the film. This supports the idea that watching violence leads to aggression, but it also supports the idea that those who tend to be more aggressive are more likely to choose to watch violence in the first place.

Evaluation

- It is possible that the questions asked beforehand had an effect on later answers, as participants could have been influenced by questions about violence while watching the film. Perhaps those who watched a violent film focused more on the violence because of the questionnaire, whereas those watching a non-violent film focused more on the lack of violence. This would be a form of **demand characteristics**.
- With questionnaires there might be **social desirability** too, and people might answer in the way they think they ought to. There may have been some respondents who realised that it is not the social norm to admit to aggression or violent behaviour, so they may not have mentioned such thoughts.

Evaluation of claimed media link to violence or crime

- Laboratory studies are reliable but not really valid, as bashing a bobo doll (Bandura), for example, is not what real violence or crime is like. The children in Bandura's work might have thought they ought to hit the doll and those in Anderson and Dill's study might also have responded as they thought they ought to (demand characteristics).

Tip

Refer to the evaluation of laboratory studies used to study witness effectiveness, as many of the evaluation points will apply here as well.

- Longitudinal studies (such as Huesmann and Eron's) follow the same group of children so are valid in that sense; however, many are likely to drop out, which can leave a biased sample. In addition, the researchers might change or leave. Another important point is that there are likely to be many changes associated with education and social norms in a culture over time, so it is hard to draw conclusions from longitudinal studies (as Huesmann and Eron did).
- Questionnaires (which Huesmann and Eron used) can lead to demand characteristics when the respondents say what they think the researcher wants. For example, parents in the Singer and Singer study may not have admitted to the actual number of hours their children watched television or indeed might not have known.
- Social learning theory suggests many role models are imitated, not just those on television, so there are many factors that can lead to aggression and crime apart from television watching. It is hard to find cause-and-effect relationships without bringing in other factors as well as the amount and/or quality of television watched (e.g. parental style or individual temperament).
- A more modern theory about the effects of television violence comes from McQuail (2002), who suggested that there were cognitive aspects of the viewer's response to what they see. Schemata for violence, which some individuals might have, are activated by violence on the screen (or in other media inputs).

Cognitions can trigger the alarm reaction (fight or flight), which is a biological response to watching violence. So the link between television violence and aggression is not just about social learning but also (perhaps) about thought patterns and cognitions.

Labelling and the self-fulfilling prophecy

Another explanation for criminal behaviour is in terms of labelling and the self-fulfilling prophecy. The idea is that first someone is labelled in a society and then the person fulfils the label and becomes what the label says. So if someone is labelled criminal in some way it is suggested that this person will become criminal. The prophecy fulfils itself.

The **self-fulfilling prophecy** (SFP) states that we become what others expect us to become. Our behaviour is received and interpreted by others, and the way they react to what we do and say affects our subsequent actions. For example, if we expect someone to be unfriendly, we behave towards him as if he is unfriendly, perhaps ignoring him. This reaction might well make the individual seem unfriendly, as he is not likely to open up to us if we are ignoring him. Thus the person behaves in an unfriendly way and the prophecy is fulfilled.

Labelling occurs when a majority group considers a minority group to be inferior and uses inferior terms when talking about them. Someone could be labelled positively ('bright'), but usually in sociology and psychology when labelling is discussed it is seen as negative. Labelling tends to come from **stereotyping** (a key term), which is where someone is seen as having characteristics of a group to which they belong (or are thought to belong). A characteristic may be observed in one member of the group and then be applied to all, or it may be a general characteristic of the group rather than something specific. Sometimes there is no direct evidence and the stereotype comes from what has been heard about the group.

The self-fulfilling prophecy comes from labelling — the individual is given a label, is treated on the basis of the label and then behaves according to it. So the behaviour then fulfils the label and the label is self-fulfilling. The SFP is often studied in schools. The prophecy has also been applied to crime. If someone is labelled as a thief and treated as one or as someone not to be trusted, then they react to expectations and behave accordingly. If we expect people to behave against social norms, and react to them in that way, they are indeed likely to fulfil that expectation.

Evidence for the self-fulfilling prophecy

Studies are used here as evidence for the SFP.

Rosenthal and Jacobson (1968)

Rosenthal and Jacobson (1968) is probably the best-known study of the SFP. They were looking at educational performance. At the start of a school year, they gave teachers some untrue information about randomly chosen pupils, saying that they were 'about to bloom' and would do well at school. They also tested the IQ of all the pupils in that class, and it was inferred that the information about the pupils came from the testing. The researchers then left the school until the end of the year, when they tested the pupils' IQ again and found that those who had been (randomly) said to be about to bloom had indeed improved more with regard to their IQ. This was true of the younger pupils in particular. It was concluded that this improvement was a result of the pupils being labelled as 'about to bloom': the teacher must have treated them in some way differently because of the label, and the pupils had fulfilled the expectations.

A problem with Rosenthal and Jacobson's study is that the effect of the SFP on educational achievement is generally thought to be small — usually teachers are correct in their predictions because they have a lot of information to draw on.

Evaluation of Rosenthal and Jacobson (1968)

Strengths	Weaknesses
• This is a well-controlled study in which the teachers did not know the IQ test results and the children said to be 'about to bloom' were randomly chosen; this deceit meant that nothing could have affected the children except for teacher attention of some sort, because they were not all 'about to bloom' • The study is replicable because it was carefully planned, so it can be tested for reliability; other studies in education have found similar results when studying teacher–child interactions	• The study is artificial and the teachers were given a false belief, which they then acted upon — perhaps they thought they were supposed to act on the information in some way, whereas in another situation, they may not have acted as they did; this is a validity problem • Perhaps it is not ethical to 'choose' some children, expecting that they will get special attention and 'bloom' when other children might not have been given special attention because of the study

CAN'T TEST – unethical to label someone a criminal incase it comes in.

Tip

When asked to evaluate studies, look at their strengths and weaknesses. One way to do this is to use GRAVE — Generalisability, Reliability, Application, Validity and Ethics.

Madon et al. (2003)

Fewer studies have been done on the SFP in relation to crime, but it is generally thought that the SFP would apply to all behaviour, not just educational improvement.

Stephanie Madon and others (2003) carried out a study to look at the effect of mothers' expectations on their children's drinking behaviour (alcohol consumption). SFP is only a problem, in the sense of needing psychological understanding, if the expectation is false. Rosenthal and Jacobson had to set up a situation using a field experiment to make sure that the expectations could be false (the pupils were randomly said to be about to bloom so it is likely that some at least were not about to bloom). Madon et al. had to find false expectations to test, and they chose to look at situations when a mother either overestimates the child's likelihood to drink or underestimates it — a naturally occurring independent variable. Mothers can have false expectations about their children's future drinking habits as they do not have much information to base their expectations on.

Madon et al. found 505 mother–child pairs, where the children came from 36 rural schools in the USA. Questionnaires and interviews were used in a longitudinal design. Questionnaires gave baseline data at first and then 18 months later were repeated. The child and the mother took part. The mother answered questions about her expectations of her child's future alcohol use and the later questionnaire asked the child for a measure of their alcohol use. The study took into account background variables, such as type of parenting, past alcohol use and self-esteem of the child, and then worked out what part of the child's use of alcohol was likely to be the result of the mother's false expectations. The expectations could be that the child would drink more than they did (18 months later) or that they would drink less than they did. The study concluded that about 52% of the relationship between the mother's expectations and the child's alcohol use (18 months later) was down to accurate expectations by the mother and 48% was down to self-fulfilling effects. It was also reported that children with high self-esteem were more susceptible to positive SFPs than those with low self-esteem. This suggests that SFPs can be more helpful, at least as they relate to positive interpersonal relationships within the family.

Evaluation

+ The study is naturalistic in that the mother's expectations are naturally occurring, so this study is possibly more valid that previous experiments (e.g. Rosenthal and Jacobson 1968).
+ It is a longitudinal design, with expectations measured first and then the child's later alcohol use, which helps by giving an element of cause and effect to the conclusions.
+ The reliability of the child's self-report data was checked to an extent.
− Even though the researchers can to a degree draw cause-and-effect conclusions because of the care in the design (longitudinal and checked for reliability), a naturalistic study showing a link between expectations and behaviour cannot scientifically measure a cause-and-effect relationship because of the many variables involved.
− In general mothers did not expect high alcohol use from their children and the children did not report high alcohol use, so the conclusions need to take this into account.

Eden (1990)

Eden (1990) found that when some soldiers selected at random were said to be of above average intelligence and others were not, those said to be intelligent did better both in written exams and in weapons tests, even though the claims about intelligence were unfounded. This suggests that there was something about the way they were treated that encouraged them in some way. This is another example of a SFP at work, though not related to crime.

Tip

Use studies that show the SFP at work, but point out that even if the study is not related to crime or antisocial behaviour it is useful to show that such a feature can explain behaviour.

content guidance

Evaluation of the SFP leading to crime

Strengths

- The SFP can be positive if expectations about behaviour are good (e.g. it predicts that if children are expected to do well, they should do so).
- Madon and other researchers found that the SFP works in areas other than education, though most research has been into education and not crime. She found factors useful when applying SFP as an explanation. For example, people with high self-esteem are more likely to be affected by parental predictions but social class does not seem to be a factor. Expectations are likely to affect criminal behaviour, but it seems that the relationship between the person having the expectations and the individual on the receiving end is important.

Weaknesses

- It seems that the SFP works if people do not know one another, but it does not work well when they know one another as they will have more information to base their expectations on. Therefore it is not easy to use just the SFP when explaining behaviour.
- Other social factors that relate to criminal behaviour can be as strong as or stronger than the SFP, which is only part of what affects behaviour. For example, child-rearing style, peer pressure or patterns of interactions within the family can affect whether a person engages in antisocial behaviour. In addition, if members of the family model antisocial behaviour, it is likely to be copied.
- As with social learning theory, there are many other factors to take into account, including relationships with others, temperament and self-esteem factors, and other learned experiences — what Madon et al. called background variables.
- A problem in studying the SFP is finding false expectations and testing them to see how far they affect the outcome.

Eyewitness testimony (three studies)

Eyewitness testimony (a key term), in the form of witness statements, is important in tracking down and convicting criminals. It refers to witness statements to the police about an incident and includes what was seen of the incident. Witnesses might be asked to identify someone in a line-up or to give evidence in a courtroom. Such statements are not as straightforward as one might think and eyewitness testimony is often thought of as unreliable, which is a key issue for society (page 38).

This section looks at three studies focusing on the reliability of eyewitness testimony. You must be able to describe and evaluate one laboratory experiment, one field study and one other study (using any methodology) in the area of eyewitness testimony. The ones chosen here are Loftus and Palmer (1974), Yuille and Cutshall (1986) and Yarmey (2004):

- Loftus and Palmer (1974) carried out a laboratory experiment looking at eyewitness testimony; their study is the compulsory study in detail in your course so it is chosen here as the laboratory experiment.

- You need one more study in detail from a list (for the studies in detail section). Yuille and Cutshall (1986) is one of the studies in the list, and, as it is a field study about eyewitness testimony, it is included here as the field study.
- The third study is a field experiment carried out by Daniel Yarmey (2004). This is chosen because it can be used as an example of a field experiment, which is required for the methodology section.

Tips
- This section covers two of the studies in detail as well as some of the required content (such as for the key issue).
- For the studies in detail section, there are two studies other than Yuille and Cutshall (1986) that you can choose from, so if you studied those in your course you might like to revise one of them instead, but make sure that overall you have a field study and a study that uses another method.
- In this guide the reliability of eyewitness testimony is chosen as the key issue as well as the area for the practical, so more information is given later about the issue. You can use your three studies when explaining and discussing the key issue.

Loftus and Palmer (1974)
Loftus and Palmer (1974) carried out two experiments within one study. This description and evaluation focuses on the first experiment as the main one.

Aims
- to see if a leading question in court is likely to affect someone's response
- to see if the phrasing of a question affects estimates of speed

Procedure
Forty-five student participants were put into groups and shown films, each involving a car accident. After each film the participants had a questionnaire to fill in. One question was critical and was about the speed of the vehicles. Some participants were asked 'How fast were the cars going when they hit each other?' and others were asked the same question but with 'hit' being replaced by 'smashed', 'collided', 'bumped' or 'contacted'. In four of the seven films the accidents were staged so the speed of the cars was known. One was travelling at 20 mph (miles per hour), two at 30 mph and one at 40 mph.

Results
- 'Smashed' gave an average estimate of 40.8 mph.
- 'Collided' gave an average estimate of 39.3 mph.
- 'Bumped' gave an average estimate of 38.1 mph.
- 'Hit' gave an average estimate of 34.0 mph.
- 'Contacted' gave an average estimate of 31.8 mph.

It can be seen that 'smashed' gave the highest estimate of speed and 'contacted' the lowest. The difference between the two was 9 mph, which is quite high.

Conclusions
- The form of the question affected the witnesses' answers.

- Perhaps estimating speeds of between 20 and 40 mph is hard and so the verbs were used to help.
- The question might have changed the memory, so that use of 'smashed' meant the crash was seen as more severe.

Evaluation of Loftus and Palmer (1974)

Strengths

- This was a laboratory experiment with clear controls — for example, they all watched the same film and were asked identical questions (except for the change of verb — the IV). Therefore the study is replicable and can be tested for reliability.
- The use of estimates of speed yielded quantitative data, so there was no interpretation from the researchers, which gave objectivity.

Weaknesses

- The student participants may not have been under the emotional strain of a real accident so there might have been a lack of validity.
- Students were used so the findings might not be generalisable to the whole population — perhaps students have different motivation when participating in the study (if this is part of the course).
- Students may have worked out what was required so there may have been demand characteristics.

Yuille and Cutshall (1986)

Aims

- to compare findings about eyewitness testimony from a real case study to findings from laboratory experiments, to check for validity
- to look at witness accounts to see how memories change (or not) some time later

Procedure

- Twenty-one witnesses to a real gun shooting were interviewed by police at the time, and the study involved returning to those witnesses some time later to see what they still remembered. Thirteen of the 21 agreed to be interviewed by the researchers. The others did not wish to take part, including the victim, who did not want to relive the trauma.
- Four or five months after the incident, 13 of the original witnesses were interviewed by the researchers and the interviews recorded and transcribed. First the witness gave their own account and then they were asked questions.
- There were two misleading questions. In one of these, half of the witnesses were asked about *a* busted headlight and half were asked about *the* busted headlight — to check Loftus and Zanni's findings (page 14). There was no broken headlight. In the other misleading question, half were asked about *the* yellow quarter panel and the other half were asked about *a* yellow quarter panel. The quarter panel was blue.
- A scoring procedure was introduced to turn the qualitative data into quantitative data.
- Some details were called 'action details' and others 'description details'. The 'description details' were divided into 'object' and 'person' details.

- The details found by Yuille and Cutshall were compared with the details found by the police earlier, so that differences in recall could be examined.

Results
- The researchers obtained more details overall (over 1,000 compared to the 650 found by the police), but they asked about information the police were not interested in, such as the colour of a blanket.
- The police found 392 action details compared with the researchers' 551.5 action details. Action details contributed around 60% of the total details found by the police, while they contributed around 52% of the total details found by the researchers.
- The police and the researchers found about the same proportion of person details (around 25%).
- The researchers found almost double the proportion of object descriptions (around 12% for the police and around 23% for the researchers).
- Witnesses varied in the number of details they recalled, but that was because they were involved in the incident to different degrees so had more or less detail to recall.
- The misleading information had little effect on the witnesses. Ten of them said there was no broken headlight and no yellow quarter panel or said they had not noticed.

Conclusions
- This was the first study of eyewitness testimony that was a field study and a study of a real case. It was useful to compare findings of this study, which was valid, with other studies (such as Loftus's) which were laboratory experiments and so tended not to be valid. The findings were different — witnesses were better at recall than found by Loftus, suggesting Loftus's findings were not valid.
- It is hard to generalise from one case study with 13 witnesses (and another 8 who did not take part).
- Eyewitnesses are not inaccurate, contrary to the findings of laboratory experiments.
- Misleading information did not lead to inaccuracies in recall.

Evaluation of Yuille and Cutshall (1986)
Strengths
- This study has validity as it is a real-life case study and a field study.
- The interviews were carried out very carefully and transcribed in great detail. Then qualitative data were transformed into quantitative data for ease of analysis and to avoid subjectivity.

Weaknesses
- Generalising from one case study to say that the findings are true of everyone might not be realistic. The study concerned a particular event which may have led to a flashbulb memory, but that might not be true of all events that witnesses have to testify about.

- Scoring was done carefully and the data were divided into details carefully. However, this is hard to do precisely and the process of changing qualitative data to quantitative data may lead to some inaccuracies.

Yarmey (2004): eyewitness recall and photo identification
Aims
- to look at the effects of a disguise on identification in a line-up
- to see if instructions to review an incident, given before an incident, would affect identification in a line-up
- to see if a time gap before identification would affect it

Procedure
There were 215 male and 375 female participants aged from 18 to 70, who were randomly assigned to different conditions (three are listed here, but there were also others):
- told that they were to be an eyewitness or not
- disguise (sunglasses and baseball cap) or not
- tested immediately or delayed by 4 hours

Actual procedure:
- Two white women were used to approach the participants and were the ones to be identified. One of the women (the target) approached a participant and asked them to help her to search for lost jewellery or asked them for directions.
- In one condition, after 2 minutes a female researcher went up to the participant and asked them to take part in the study. They then either asked them there and then to identify the woman target or asked them 4 hours later.
- Witnesses were also given a questionnaire asking about the woman who had approached them (the target). They were asked about her clothing and physical characteristics.
- Then they were given a set of six photos. In half of the cases the target woman was among the six photos and in the other half she was not.
- In a different part of the study students were given the scenarios (a target woman approaching a participant and so on) and were asked what they thought would happen.
- At the end of the study there was a debriefing.

Results
There were many conditions, so the results are complex. The following points give some of them:
- When the target was in the photo line-up (of six photos) she was identified by about 49% of the participants.
- When the women was not in the photos 62% of the participants correctly said she was not there.
- The students who were asked what would happen thought that only about 47% would correctly say that the woman was not there, so one result is that people (in this case the students) misjudge what an eyewitness will get right or wrong. The

students underestimated the participants' ability to say that the woman was not there.

- 63% of the students thought that when the target's photo was in the line-up the witness would pick it out, whereas in the study only 49% correctly picked it out when it was there — so the students overestimated what an eyewitness would 'remember'.
- The participants who were prepared for the test (told beforehand) were better at recall (questionnaire data) but not better at picking the photo out of the line-up.
- Age estimates were more accurate than height or weight estimates.

Conclusions
- About 50% of the time a witness makes a correct identification if the target is in the line-up.
- The findings correspond with those of another study — a meta-analysis by Haber and Haber (2001) — so each study supports the other.
- A practical application is that jurors are likely to overestimate an eyewitness's ability to recall and to pick out a person from a line-up, so such testimony should be questioned.

Evaluation of Yarmey (2004)
Strengths
- The photo line-up findings support Haber and Haber (2001), which suggests there is reliability in the study. Both studies found witnesses tend to be about 50% accurate in a line-up identification when the target is present in the line-up.
- The study has ecological validity (as field experiments tend to) because the target approached participants in their natural setting and (except in one condition) the participants were unaware that they were part of a study until after the meeting.
- The study was carefully controlled so it is replicable and can be tested for reliability.
- There was a large age range and good male/female balance, so there is likely to be good generalisability of the findings.

Weaknesses
- Yuille and Cutshall (1986) found that witnesses were accurate with regard to height and weight whereas Yarmey (2004) found they were accurate with regard to age, so the findings of the two studies differ, which suggests a lack of reliability.
- A photo line-up is not the same as a real line-up, and only faces were shown in the photos, so the study to that extent lacked validity.
- Not all eyewitnesses who have to give evidence or identify a target have been approached and asked a question by the target, so perhaps generalisation should only be to similar situations.

Methods of treating offenders

This section focuses on two ways of treating offenders. There are, of course, other ways of treating crime and other initiatives that might help to prevent it — the examples considered here are only some of the ways psychology investigates these areas. In this unit guide, **token economy** (a key term) and anger management programmes are the two chosen treatments.

> **Tip**
>
> You may have covered token economy and one other treatment programme (not anger management), so you could choose to revise that one instead.

Token economy programmes

Token economy programmes (TEPs) have been used to help control aggression in institutions. They involve operant conditioning principles. The idea is that aggressive behaviour is maladaptive and needs to be changed. The aim is to replace the aggressive behaviour with more appropriate behaviour. More appropriate behaviour is identified and might involve, for example, being polite to others or taking part in a team activity calmly. Once the required behaviour is identified, instances of it are rewarded. The individual is given tokens for this approved behaviour and the tokens can be exchanged for something desirable, such as visits or television watching.

The tokens are not themselves reinforcing — it is what they buy that is reinforcing. The required behaviour is rewarded and the maladaptive aggressive behaviour is not, so the theory is that the required behaviour will replace the maladaptive behaviour. It is possible that as part of the programme the maladaptive behaviour is punished too. Alternatively, **negative reinforcement** can be used to stop the unwanted behaviour; for example, privileges can be removed if that behaviour is displayed.

One early TEP was set up in the USA by Teodoro Ayllon. The programme lasted a year and involved adolescents who were rewarded for required behaviour. This was the programme that started the use of TEPs.

Studies evaluating TEPs

Milby (1975) found that TEPs were successful in psychiatric hospitals in controlling behaviour, but felt that more should be done to investigate their use alongside drug programmes. The programmes seemed to work outside the hospital as well but Milby thought more follow-up studies were needed.

For schizophrenia, Dickerson et al. (2003) found that TEPs were successful at obtaining the required behaviour, but they thought (like Milby) that it was necessary to know more about how the programmes worked alongside medication. It was also thought that more studies were needed now as the original programmes were started in the 1970s.

> **Tip**
>
> Studies evaluating TEPs can be used even if they do not involve crime or antisocial behaviour, as is done here, but make sure that you explain how their findings can also apply to such behaviour. Your answer should always focus on the relevant applicant.

Field et al. (2004) looked at the treatment of young people with behavioural problems, involving TEPs and group work, and found that there were some young people who did not respond, although in general the programmes worked. If those who did not respond were given more immediate and more frequent rewards, they responded more. This suggests that the pattern of rewards must suit the individual and that design of the programme is important in its success.

> **Tip**
>
> TEPs use learning theory principles and fall within the learning approach. The programme is a contribution of the approach to society — to help in treating criminals. You will need to know about TEPs in Unit 4, when you are asked for a therapy or treatment from the learning approach in clinical psychology, and when you look at social control for the section on issues and debates.

Evaluation of TEPs

> **Tip**
>
> In this unit guide, strengths and weaknesses of a study or a theory are often indicated using + (plus) and − (minus) symbols, but do not use these in the examination. Use full sentences and make your point clearly, including whether it is a strength or a weakness.

Strengths and weaknesses of TEPs

Strengths	Weaknesses
• Can be administered by anyone (with training) and tokens and rewards are relatively cheap, so the programme is not expensive and there are more benefits than costs • Have been found to be successful by many studies, even though there tends to be 10–20% of people who do not respond well to TEPs	• Learning might not transfer to the home environment, so there might be recidivism • Programmes have to be carefully planned and controlled, and there are many areas where problems can occur (such as lack of consistency from staff) • Other prisoners also reinforce behaviour, and the behaviour they reinforce is likely to be different from that required by staff • Few long-term studies have been done to see if the effects of the programme last once the individual is released from prison

Anger management programmes

Anger management programmes focus on cognitive processes and can help to control aggression. The aim of such programmes is to assist individuals in recognising thoughts that precede an aggressive attack and then changing those thoughts. The idea is that thoughts lead to anger, and that the release of tension via anger will relieve pressure. Therefore, individuals learn to become angry, as that anger successfully relieves their tension.

The three stages of anger control programmes are as follows:

(1) **Cognitive preparation** — where individuals learn to recognise thoughts that precede anger.

(2) **Skills acquisition** — where individuals learn self-control through self-talk. Social skills training or assertiveness training can be useful here. The focus is on behaviour or control of thoughts that will successfully turn people away from their learned aggressive responses. Social skills training involves modelling, instructing and role play.

(3) **Application practice** — where situations are set up so that individuals can practise becoming aware of their thoughts and overcoming the aggression that follows.

Anger management programmes can be one-to-one but more often are carried out in groups. Programmes can focus on relaxation as well as social skills training and learning to spot triggers. Outbursts, as angry episodes are called when they lead to aggression that can be criminal (e.g. crimes against the person and grievous bodily harm), can come from learned patterns of behaviour, so the focus is also on replacing learned maladaptive behaviour with more suitable behaviour.

Tip

Anger management programmes tend to link to the cognitive approach, as suggested by the description above, but there are elements of the learning approach as well, such as the use of modelling and positive reinforcement. You might need to use a treatment from the cognitive approach for clinical psychology and/or the issues and debates section (Unit 4), so knowledge of anger management programmes will be useful there.

An example of an anger management programme — CALM

CALM is a registered name and stands for Controlling Anger and Learning to Manage. The programme teaches participants to monitor and understand their emotions so that they can prevent problematic behaviour. The necessary skills to reduce the intensity and frequency of the outbursts are focused on. The CALM programme is designed for adult and adolescent males who are at risk of recidivism (going back to criminal behaviour). The programme uses modelling, role play, teamwork, self-evaluation, peer evaluation and personal assignments.

Studies evaluating anger management programmes

Watt et al. (1999) in Western Australia looked at cognitive–behavioural anger management programmes for violent offenders, comparing violent male offenders on the programme with offenders on a waiting list but not on the programme (as a control). Measures taken included anger knowledge, anger expression, observed aggressive behaviour and misconduct in prison. There seemed to be no gain for those on the treatment programme compared with those on the waiting list.

Towl and Dexter (1994) evaluated nine anger management programmes in England and Wales, using self-report questionnaires. Prisoners reported a drop in anger at the end of the programmes, though it was found that six of the prisoners had an extreme drop in anger and the others showed little difference, so the findings were not very conclusive.

Ireland (2000) looked at 50 young offenders and found a reduction in their anger after the programme.

Evaluation of anger management programmes

- McDougall et al. (1987) found that offences were reduced when 18 young offenders who were in prison underwent an anger control programme.
- Goldstein et al. (1989) found that 15% of those who had undergone an anger control programme and social skills training reoffended, whereas 43% of a control group were arrested again.
- Goldstein (1986) found in a review of studies of social skills training that skills such as those involving eye contact and negotiation with others had been learned.
- Losel (1995) considered 500 studies of such programmes and found that, overall, there was a 10% drop in reoffending (recidivism), which suggests that these programmes work at least to some extent.
- Studies showing the success of the programmes gathered self-report data from the prisoners themselves so the findings are likely to be valid.
- For the programme to work, individuals must be able to focus on their own thoughts and their aggression must stem from anger.
- Even if the programme works in a prison setting, its success may not be transferred once the offenders return to their own environments.
- Many studies do not continue long enough to predict recidivism.

Studies in detail

You need to cover two studies in detail. Loftus and Palmer (1974) and Yuille and Cutshall (1986) have been described and evaluated on pages 30–33.

Evidence in practice: key issue and practical

Key issue

The key issue chosen here is the reliability of eyewitness memory. You need to be able to describe what the problem is with regard to the reliability of eyewitness testimony — in particular that it may be unreliable. Witness testimony is used in court to convict people of crimes and such convictions clearly need to be based on solid evidence. If witness testimony is unreliable — not because witnesses are lying but because of features of memory and the situation — then there is an important issue to be addressed. Convictions made solely on the basis of unreliable information need to be overturned, and some have been.

> **Tips**
> - Eyewitness testimony may have been the key issue you studied for the cognitive approach at AS. If so, recall that information now, so that this section builds on what you have already learned.

- There are other key issues that you can choose, so if you studied one of those in your course you might like to revise that one instead. It is best to choose your own key issue to revise as you will have carried out your own practical and will have to answer questions on it.

Theory on problems with eyewitness memory

Problems with eyewitness memory might arise due to the various factors discussed below.

Length of time of the incident

One problem is estimating the time an incident lasts for. This tends to be overestimated (Buckhout 1974).

Confidence levels of witnesses

Witnesses can be more confident than the situation warrants.

- Clark and Stephenson (1995) asked policemen to recall an incident. Some policemen were alone, some were in pairs and some were in groups of four. All were confident about their recall, with the groups of four being the most accurate, and the most confident — even when wrong.

Attention at encoding

Attention when encoding the information is a problem as we cannot attend to everything at once, and it is likely that we do not know we are going to be called upon as a witness of an incident, so we will not necessarily attend to what is needed.

- Buckhout (1980) showed how inaccurate the memory of an eyewitness can be. Television viewers watched a mugging in a New York street and then saw a line-up of six people, including the mugger. The viewers then telephoned in to identify the mugger, with only 14% accuracy.

Problems with accessing memories

Strong associations between objects and events may be more easily recalled from long-term memory than weak associations. Incorrect memories can arise from making the wrong associations.

Arousal

The level of arousal can affect recall, and in events where we are eyewitnesses we are likely to be highly aroused. Memories are said to be inaccurate when we are aroused (Hollin 1989).

- Loftus et al. (1983) showed some participants a film featuring a fire and showed others a less emotional event. When those who watched the fire were reminded of it, they had worse recall. Perhaps the emotion of the event disrupted their recall.

The weapon focus effect

The weapon focus effect might be linked to arousal.

- Loftus et al. (1987) found that if a weapon was present in a situation, people tended to focus on the weapon — or at least they had poorer recall for faces in these situations.

- Mitchell et al. (1998) suggested that Loftus et al.'s findings were not due to arousal, as even when someone was holding a stick of celery and not a weapon, people focused on that. Perhaps it was that the celery or weapon simply drew people's attention — either was unusual and so was attended to.

Leading questions that bias retrieval

Quite a lot of research has been done in this area, including the following studies:

- Loftus (1978) showed 195 participants a slide: 95 of them saw a small red Datsun car at a stop sign and 100 saw the car at a give way sign. They saw other slides too. Later in the test, they were asked questions about what they had seen: one questionnaire included a question about a car at a stop sign, while another questionnaire had a question about a car at a give way sign. This meant that some participants had a question that was consistent with what they had seen, and some had a question that was not. Of those given a consistent question (e.g. asking about a stop sign when they had seen a stop sign), 75% had accurate recall, compared with 41% for those given an inconsistent question. This suggests that an inconsistent question can bias our recall.
- Garry et al. (1994) used two brothers in a study. They asked the older brother to tell his 14-year-old younger brother that the younger brother had been lost in a shopping mall when he was a small child. The older brother gave his younger brother correct information as well, and then incorporated the story of being lost in with the rest. When the 14-year-old was asked about the incident 2 weeks later, he recalled being lost and included other information too, which he seemed to have added to the 'memory'.

Evaluation

- The experiments involved careful controls and the findings have been replicated.
- The findings of the various studies support one another.
- In the Garry et al. study, a false memory was implanted, so the ethics of this study should be questioned. This is particularly important as the participant was only 14 years old.
- Loftus (1997) emphasised that only peripheral information (such as whether a sign was a stop sign or a give way sign) had distorted recall. Central information may be recalled more accurately. For example, when a study was done that involved a red purse being stolen, and the colour was distinctive, 98% of participants recalled the colour of the purse.
- It may be that a memory itself is accurate, but misleading questions affect retrieval of the memory, although it is hard to test this.
- Experiments are often not valid as the situations are not natural. In real-life events, the witness would be a participant in a different sense.

Theory on how to improve eyewitness testimony

Shapiro and Penrod (1986)

Shapiro and Penrod (1986) suggested that there is improved recall if the situation where recall takes place is similar to the setting of the incident. This suggests that victim or witness recall will be assisted by setting up a similar situation or by helping to recreate the situation mentally. It also seems to help both witness and victim memories if evidence is given quite soon after the event.

Cognitive interviews

Police have acted on this research and use cognitive interviews to help the witness to set the scene again and recreate the situation mentally. Police are also made aware of biases such as those outlined above. Cognitive interviews focus on the idea of context reinstatement and giving the witness cues that might trigger memories. It is essential that the witness talks about everything, not just what is thought to be important by police interviewers or the witness.

Changing perspective may be helpful — the witness is asked to imagine what another witness may have seen, for example. This can help to avoid too much interpretation on the part of the witness, such as bias that might be introduced by causes which the witness attributes to certain events that took place. Changing the order of events may also be helpful — the witness is asked about what happened before the incident, or to work backwards through it.

These various techniques can help to break down biases. Other important techniques include helping witnesses to relax and letting them do the talking. If the interviewer guides the questions too much, puts pressure on the witness or does not pick up on the focus of the responses, something might easily be missed.

> **Tip**
>
> Use the 'theory' information above when applying concepts and ideas from your learning to explain the issue of unreliability of eyewitness testimony.

Practical — carrying out an analysis of two articles

An example of how to do this practical can be found in the 'Getting Started' booklet that accompanies the course and comes with the specification. This information can be found on the Edexcel website if you need to access it. However, you should use your own practical for this section as you will need to answer questions based on what you did.

Child psychology
Definition of the application

Child psychology is about a child's development and various aspects of the developing child. The focus is on social, emotional and cognitive development. Not only is typical child development studied but also abnormal development, and the emphasis is often on problems faced by children. The United Nations Convention on the Rights of the Child (1989) defines childhood as being from birth to the age of 18, so 'child' includes teenagers, although child psychology more often than not focuses on infants and young children.

Key terms you might be asked about are defined in this content section as they arise: attachment (page 49), deprivation (page 49), separation anxiety (page 49), evolution (page 51), privation (page 57), and daycare (page 62).

> **Tip**
>
> A good way to extend a definition, when 3 marks are available, is to add an example. When defining child psychology you will be able to give examples from the content section as well, such as the focus on autism.

Methodology/how science works

This section looks at naturalistic observations, structured observations, case studies, cross-cultural studies and longitudinal studies.

> **Tip**
>
> You have studied observations as part of your study of the learning approach, and case studies and longitudinal studies as part of the psychodynamic approach. Recall what you learned there.

You will look at a case study when you cover Genie's story (Curtiss 1977), and you will look at structured observations and cross-cultural studies when you study the strange situation procedure and attachment behaviour. Use your learning as examples in the methodology section.

Naturalistic observations
- **Naturalistic observations** take place in the participants' natural setting.
- They can be **participant observations** (the researcher is involved in the situation) or **non-participant observations** (the researcher remains apart from the situation).
- They can be **overt** (the participants are aware that they are taking part in the study and informed of the details) or **covert** (the participants are not aware that they are taking part).
- They can gather **quantitative** data if categories are developed and **tallying** used.
- They can gather **qualitative** data if recordings and sometimes **transcripts** are made — so that all the detail is gathered.
- **Inter-observer reliability** can be checked by having more than one observer (trained with regard to what they are recording, and recording in the same situation) and correlating the findings of the different observers.
- An example of a naturalistic observation in child psychology is Parten's (1932) study of play behaviour, where she found different types of play according to a child's age.

> **Tip**
>
> Make sure you do not describe a research method using bullet points like those above (though useful for study and revision, they are not appropriate in examination answers).

Naturalistic observations in child psychology

- Parten (1932) looked at play and found different types according to a child's age. She watched free-play sessions, which meant the children were allowed to choose what they played with and how they spent the time.
- Patterson (1982) recorded parent–child interactions in detail, using naturalistic observation to understand what triggers led to particular behaviours.
- Melhuish et al. (1990) used naturalistic observations as part of their study of young children looking at the effects of different types of daycare. This was a longitudinal study and involved interviews and questionnaires as well. They studied 18-month-old children to see how type of care affected their behaviour. There were four groups — one group had no daycare but stayed with their mothers (the home group), another group was cared for in a day nursery, a third was with a childminder and the fourth group was with relatives. The study found that the home and relatives groups were more responsive than the nursery group and that aggression was greater in nurseries but low overall. There were other findings as well. It was concluded that different types of daycare give different outcomes.

> **Evaluation of Melhuish et al. (1990)**
>
> + There was inter-observer reliability.
> + The children were observed during free play so they could choose their own activities, which made comparisons between the groups fair.
> – The nurseries were private ones and not well resourced. The same findings might not be made in different types of nursery.
> – Observations were of 18-month-olds so the findings might not generalise to other age groups.

Evaluation of naturalistic observations, including reliability, validity and ethics

- Naturalistic observations are reliable if inter-observer reliability is carefully established by using more than one observer and carrying out tests to check that the data correspond. They are less reliable if the data are qualitative as it is hard to repeat the whole study with the same situation and so on. They may not be reliable if participant observation is used, as a researcher who is involved in the situation may not capture all the data.
- They are valid in that they take place in the natural setting so there is ecological validity. Perhaps they are not valid when they are overt as the participants are aware of being observed and that may affect their behaviour.
- Naturalistic observations are ethical in that they do not involve manipulating variables or putting the participant in any situation they are not used to. If they are overt, informed consent can be gained and the right to withdraw given.

However, they are not ethical if covert because the participant cannot be forewarned — they would then lack informed consent and the right to withdraw. Often the individual being observed cannot be asked for permission, so observations are said to be ethical if they take place in a public setting where people would expect to be observed.

- There can be observer drift when observers drift away from what they have planned.

Summary of the strengths and weaknesses of naturalistic observations

Strengths	Weaknesses
• Valid because in natural setting, so natural behaviour observed	• Not valid in that there is an observer, so the behaviour might be affected
• Reliable because tallying, time sampling, prepared categories and more than one observer can give inter-observer reliability	• Not valid because of observer drift, where observers move away from the plan
	• Not reliable because observation is at one time, in one situation, with particular observers, and the same situation is not likely to recur

Structured observations

Structured observations are those made in a situation set up with careful controls, instead of in a natural situation. All experiments are likely to involve gathering data by observing what happens, but in a structured situation the main way of gathering data is by observing what happens without strict control over the IV and without the DV being measured in any other way. Bandura watched the behaviour of the children with the Bobo doll, but this was called a laboratory experiment because of the manipulation of the IV, the operationalisation of the DV and the many controls. In a structured observation there is structure but not a carefully manipulated IV.

Structured observations in child psychology

One example of a structured observation in child psychology is the **strange situation test** developed by Ainsworth (page 54). Structured observations are also used when applying child psychology to situations: for example, an educational psychologist may set up structured observations to investigate interactions with a teacher.

Evaluation of structured observations, including validity, reliability and ethical issues

- They can be tested for reliability thanks to their structure.
- They are effective with regard to cost and time, because the situation of interest (such as a young child being left alone with a stranger) might not be observed for some time if it is not set up.

- The situations are set up rather than natural, so there may not be validity.
- There might be demand characteristics in that the participants may work out what is required.
- They may not be ethical; for example, in the strange situation test the child is likely to become upset (though the mother is in control and can re-enter the room or stop the study whenever she wishes to).

Ethical issues in research with children

There are special ethical guidelines for use when working with children, and these are published by the British Psychological Society. For example, parents give consent but it is now common to ask the children not only for consent but also to be more involved in the study.

Case studies

- **Case studies** are in-depth studies, usually of single individuals, or sometimes of a small group.
- They tend to involve many different research methods to gather plenty of rich detailed material.
- In this way **triangulation** can be used to test for reliability and validity — this means comparing the data from different sources to see if they correspond, in which case there is validity and reliability.
- Data tend to be qualitative to allow in-depth analysis; however, as many different research methods are likely to be used, there can be quantitative data as well.
- Case studies tend to include case background — information about the person or small group, including their upbringing, culture, experiences, family background, specific experiences and perhaps trauma.
- Case studies focus on case description and case analysis, rather than procedure and results, because the description of the situation and the analysis of it can be hard to separate.
- Case studies tend to have an aim rather than a hypothesis, because they focus on finding out as much as possible about an individual or small group, rather than on testing a specific aspect with controls in place for all other aspects of the situation.
- An example of a case study is Curtiss's (1977) study of Genie, a child who had been very badly treated and had not been socialised before she was discovered at the age of around 13 years.

Tip

When giving an example to illustrate a research method, make sure you give more than the name of the study, to show that you both know and understand the study.

Evaluation of case studies

Summary of the strengths and weaknesses of case studies

Strengths	Weaknesses
• They are reliable to an extent, because the same data can be found from different research methods	• They are of a unique individual in particular circumstances, so are hard to replicate to test for reliability
• They tend to be valid because they often take place in the real-life setting of the individual or small group	• For the same reasons they are not generalisable

Case studies in child psychology

The study of Genie by Curtiss (1977) was a case study (page 59) which gathered information from as many sources as possible and was then written up in detail. For example, the case background was detailed as far as possible, with as much information as was known about Genie from her birth. After Genie was found, her behaviour was documented thoroughly both at the hospital and when she moved on to live in people's houses. Film was used, and notes were kept to record certain behaviours as they occurred and were then written up.

Another case study is Freud's study of Little Hans, which was within the psychodynamic approach and focused on Hans's background and development. Freud's case studies tended to focus specifically on uncovering unconscious thoughts.

Dibs, a case study written up by Axline, was also within the psychodynamic approach because it considered treatment of Dibs using play therapy and focused on how repressed feelings were affecting Dibs's behaviour.

Case studies in child psychology often focus on children with problems so that they can be understood and possibly helped. Little Hans needed treatment for a phobia of horses, Dibs needed treatment for 'silence' and difficult behaviour, and Genie needed treatment in the form of socialising. However, case studies can also be carried out to investigate child development in general. Takei (2001) did a study in Japan on how sign language develops in deaf children, looking at two children in detail to code their signs and explain how their language progressed.

Evaluation of case studies used in child psychology

- Case studies are useful for child psychologists and educational psychologists when focusing on a child whose development is problematic for some reason, as the detail that is needed could not be gathered in any other way.
- Case studies are often **longitudinal** so are useful in showing developmental changes, which is also often necessary in child psychology, not only to learn about how children develop but also to follow a treatment programme to monitor its success.
- However, case studies focus on one individual or a small group so their findings are not easily generalisable to others. For example, Genie was unique — even

though other children have, sadly, been found in very bad conditions in similar ways, each child has had unique experiences so it is uncertain that findings about one can apply to another.

Evaluating case studies in terms of reliability, validity and ethics

- It is hard to show reliability with case studies because they are not replicable. Little Hans, once treated for his phobia, would not be the same again to study. However, there can sometimes be tests for reliability if data are gathered using different research methods or different people. For example, different psychologists worked with Genie, so if they all claimed that her language developed a little but not fully then this finding could be said to be reliable.

- Case studies tend to be valid because they involve the participant so thoroughly and the data clearly come from the participant. For example, film of Genie shows her use of language clearly, and the validity of claims that she has language difficulties is not in doubt. However, as with all studies in psychology, there is some interpretation if only in the data chosen for inclusion — so to an extent there might be a lack of validity. Additionally, it is often claimed that Genie was **privated** (very badly treated and with no attachment figure from the start) and had very poor language skills, and argued that, therefore, being privated causes poor language skills. However, it is possible that Genie had some difficulties from birth that led to poor language development. The conclusion might not be valid.

- Case studies are likely to be ethical because the in-depth study can be explained to the participant, who can be involved throughout. The participant can check the validity of the data and can influence what is included so there can be both informed consent and right to withdraw. However, case studies of children, or of vulnerable adults, might not be so ethical. It could be claimed that Genie was given no choice about her treatment, and she was studied as well as treated — the two were muddled up. Questions have been asked about the ethics of the Genie study. Little Hans too was put forward for study by his parents — perhaps not an ethical thing to do.

> **Tip**
>
> The three issues (reliability, validity and ethics) have been fully explained above to show that you need to make your points clearly and with sufficient detail. You are not likely to get marks for saying 'case studies are valid', for example. In this unit guide, where the goal is to summarise information, such detail is not always provided, but be sure to give it in an examination answer.

Cross-cultural studies

In **cross-cultural studies**, studies are carried out in more than one culture and their findings compared, in order to find differences or similarities between cultures. Some of these studies are detailed in the 'content' section (page 56). Cross-cultural studies can use any methodology as long as they involve both carrying out the study in different cultures and comparing the findings between cultures.

Evaluating cross-cultural studies as a methodology

Summary of the strengths and weaknesses of cross-cultural procedures

Strengths	Weaknesses
• Cross-cultural procedures are a main way of studying nature and nurture issues • There is likely to be reliability when procedures are carefully controlled, so they can be repeated • Ethnographic cross-cultural studies are valid and in depth	• There is a lack of validity in transferring a procedure from one culture to another, as there are likely to be different understandings of what the procedure is and how to react to it • There is a lack of validity in setting up a procedure that is controlled enough to be repeated in different cultures • If case studies and ethnographic methods are used, they are likely to be more valid, but they might be hard to compare and to generalise from

Longitudinal studies

Longitudinal studies are those which follow the participant(s) over a period of time to look for developmental changes or assess the effects of a treatment that is carried out over time. They are used in most areas of psychology. You may have covered the longitudinal study by Huesmann and Eron (1986) (page 24) in criminological psychology.

For child psychology two longitudinal studies are discussed in the 'content' section (pages 62–63); these investigate the effects of daycare on children (EPPE and NICHD). The study of Genie (page 59) was also a longitudinal one.

Evaluation of longitudinal studies

Summary of the strengths and weaknesses of longitudinal ways of studying children

Strengths	Weaknesses
• Uses the same people, so there is good control over participant variables • Only age changes, so strong conclusions can be drawn about how people develop over time	• Many factors change over time as well as age, so picking out particular cause-and-effect conclusions is difficult • The likely high drop-out rate can lead to a biased sample

Content

There are quite a few theories and studies to cover in child psychology and these are necessarily kept short in the revision material presented here. The major subsections deal with the following: Bowlby's theory of attachment and maternal deprivation (including evidence from various sources); ideas of how negative effects of deprivation and separation can be reduced; evaluation of Bowlby's ideas; Ainsworth's strange situation test and studies of attachment; research into privation; daycare and its effects on children; and autism.

Bowlby's theory of attachment and maternal deprivation

- Bowlby worked as a psychiatrist within the psychodynamic approach, focusing on loss and on children who were maladjusted or delinquent.
- He thought that early relationships with parents could cause later problems for the child and used psychodynamic concepts, such as the idea that the mother acted as ego and superego for the child until the child developed sufficiently.
- He wrote a report for the World Health Organization focusing on the importance of the mother–child attachment and a single attachment for the child, which he called **monotropy**. The attachment figure could be someone other than the child's mother, though at that time (1951) mothers were the most likely attachment figures.
- Monotropy refers to a warm and loving relationship with one person.
- Bowlby's idea was that if the mother–child bond was broken early in life this would lead to problems with social, emotional and intellectual development — this was the **maternal deprivation hypothesis**.
- Bowlby suggested that such problems — following maternal deprivation — were irreversible and once they had developed they could not be put right.
- **Deprivation** (a key term) occurs when someone has a warm, continuous, loving relationship with one person (an attachment) and is deprived of it through some sort of separation (which can be long term or short term). This could happen, for example, if a child goes into hospital or if their mother or attachment figure goes into hospital. Daycare can also be seen as short-term separation and so is deprivation to an extent.
- **Attachment** (a key term) refers to a warm, continuous, loving relationship with a person who provides a safe haven and secure base from which to explore.
- **Separation anxiety** (a key term) is displayed by infants from around 7 or 8 months, in that they will cling to their attachment figure if a stranger tries to interact with them and will be distressed by separation from their attachment figure. This shows that a secure attachment is in place.
- Such ideas led to changes in institutions such as allowing parental visiting rights, which were not allowed before.

Bowlby's own evidence — the 44 Juvenile Thieves study (1944)

Bowlby's study of 44 children is a study in detail for the course. It is described and evaluated over the next pages so that it can be used here as evidence and also for the 'studies in detail' section later on, where it is only referred to.

Aims

- The study was to find out about the background of young people who came to see Bowlby in his capacity as a psychiatrist, to determine if he could establish the reason for them becoming thieves.
- The study was to investigate why some young people become delinquents.

Procedure

- The study was carried out from 1936 to 1939 in the London Child Guidance Clinic and used interviews, case histories and psychological testing to look for patterns in the backgrounds of young people at the clinic.
- When children came to the clinic they were given mental tests to measure intelligence and were also assessed for their emotional attitudes. Bowlby was interested in social, emotional and intellectual development.
- A social worker used a 1-hour interview to log the child's history and Bowlby then interviewed both the child and the mother. The information given by the mother helped him establish whether the child had experienced separation in early life and for how long. A case conference was held to reach an initial diagnosis and then further data were gathered using more interviews.
- This was not so much an academic study as an assessment for treatment, though the data were then used to draw 'academic' conclusions.
- Only a few case studies were used, as it was time-consuming to log and collect the data. Bowlby's study would be improved by having a similar amount of data about children who were not at the clinic. The 44 children studied were referred to the clinic by several agencies for various reasons, 22 of them by the child's school. There was a control group of 44 children who were at the clinic but not thieves.

Results

- The average intelligence of the thieves and the control group was quite high and about a third of each group were of above average intelligence.
- Of the thieves, 15 were under 9 years old and half under 11, though only one child under 11 had been charged.
- There were 31 boys and 13 girls in the main group and 34 boys and 10 girls in the control group. The clinic usually had 60% boys and 40% girls so the groups were not representative.
- In 22 cases there was serious stealing over a long time and for 7 children the stealing had lasted for more than 3 years. However, 8 thieves had only been involved in a few thefts and 4 had only been involved in one theft.
- Bowlby sorted the thieves into six types of character. Of the 44 thieves, 42 had an abnormal character type. The study outlines in detail all the character types but only Group E, the affectionless type, is considered here as it is the one of interest in this context.
- **Affectionless** means having a lack of normal affection, shame or sense of responsibility.
- Fourteen of the children had an affectionless character — a lack of warmth or feeling for anyone. Bowlby thought that such children had experienced emotional

loss of their mother or primary caregiver early in their lives and that this had affected their character. Misery was behind the mask.

- There were no affectionless characters in the control group.

Conclusions

93% of the affectionless thieves (13 out of the 14) were at a high level of stealing and 56% of the persistent thieves (those at a high level of stealing) were affectionless. This seemed conclusive evidence that affectionless psychopathy can lead to stealing and, more generally and importantly, that suffering emotional loss of mother early in life leads to antisocial behaviour and emotional problems.

Evaluation of Bowlby's thieves study

Strengths

- A lot of in-depth and detailed data were gathered using different research methods, and both qualitative and quantitative data were collected, so the data are likely to be valid if they agree with one another.
- There was a matched control group of children who were also in the clinic but were not thieves, which provided a useful baseline measure.

Weaknesses

- Bowlby would have liked a control group of typically developing children as well as the group of thieves and the clinic control group, because the latter were perhaps not typically developing children.
- Bowlby looked at aspects of social, emotional and intellectual development, but not at other features in development such as relationship with father and other family members and experience in school.

Lorenz's work and Bowlby's theory about the evolutionary basis of attachment

- Bowlby thought that a child's need for an attachment figure was an evolutionary trait. He used Lorenz's work as evidence.
- Lorenz (1952) found that geese would follow the first moving object they saw after birth. **Imprinting** is the term for this following behaviour. The first moving object seen would normally be the mother, but when Lorenz made sure it was him instead, they followed him (imprinted on him).
- Lorenz concluded that the young geese that followed the mother would have survived, so the ones with that trait lived and passed those genes on.
- Bowlby used this idea to suggest that attaching was a survival trait. This is about **evolution** (a key term): genes that help the organism survive are passed on through reproduction whereas characteristics that do not aid survival die out because the genes for those characteristics are not passed on through reproduction (the organism does not survive to reproduce).

Evaluation of Lorenz's findings

Strengths

- There is validity with regard to the behaviour of geese, because Lorenz used ethology — the study of animals in their natural setting.

- Later experiments replicated the findings. For example, when a rubber glove was used, the geese duly followed it because it was the first moving object they saw.

Weaknesses
- Only some animals show imprinting behaviour, which suggests it cannot be used as a universal law of behaviour.
- It might not be legitimate to generalise from animals to humans because of the obvious differences.

Harlow's work as evidence for the importance of attachment
- Harlow (with others) studied rhesus monkeys to look at the effects of removing any attachment figure from them.
- Harlow and Zimmerman (1959) removed infant monkeys from their mothers and allowed them access to two 'monkeys' made of wire. One monkey was purely wire and they could feed from it; the other monkey was covered in towelling so it was soft and could offer comfort. There were other infant monkeys who could only access the wire monkey. It was found that when possible the monkeys ran to the towel-covered monkey so they did not just want food from their 'mother' but also comfort. This was taken as evidence that babies need attachment and comfort, not just food.

Evaluation of the Harlow and Zimmerman (1959) study
Strengths
- The findings seem valid as films showed the monkeys clearly frightened and running to the towel-covered monkey.
- Monkeys were used and they share 98% or more of their genes with humans, so there can be generalisation to humans to an extent.
- Schaffer and Emerson (1964) found that infants formed multiple attachments, showing that infants do not just attach to their mothers for food. This reinforces the Harlow and Zimmerman findings.

Weaknesses
- Animals are not the same as humans so generalisation is not really valid.
- Ethically Harlow and Zimmerman's work is questioned because the monkeys were so clearly distressed whereas animals should suffer as little as possible — and the studies were repeated perhaps more than was necessary.

Robertson's naturalistic observations to show importance of attachment
- James Robertson, who was part of Bowlby's team, carried out a detailed observation of a 2-year-old's stay in hospital.
- The observation was filmed and the study of 'Laura' had an important influence on the decision to allow parents into hospitals, because of her visible distress at being in the hospital.
- Robertson recorded three stages of deprivation — protest (the child cries and can show anger and fear as well), despair (the child is clearly very distressed and cries a lot) and finally detachment (the child seems to settle down and stops crying).

- The detachment phase was thought to involve depression more than acceptance.

Evaluating Robertson's research

Strengths
- Naturalistic observations give valid data.
- Robertson filmed other children in similar situations with similar responses, so the findings were replicated.

Weaknesses
- Naturalistic observations are hard to replicate as they are specific to one situation and often to one person, so reliability is in doubt.
- Naturalistic observations are hard to generalise from, as they are specific to one situation and often to one person, so are unique.

Ideas of how negative effects of deprivation and separation can be reduced

Bowlby studied deprivation, and evidence presented in this unit guide includes his own Juvenile Thieves study, Lorenz's study of geese, Harlow's work with deprived rhesus monkeys and James Robertson's observations of children in hospital settings. Later, in discussing daycare (which involves deprivation and separation), more evidence is offered about the negative effects of deprivation and how they can be reduced.

The negative effects of deprivation

Evidence has been presented in this unit guide for the following negative effects of deprivation:
- affectionless psychopathy
- three stages of protest, despair and detachment
- problems with social, emotional and intellectual development
- difficulties with relationships (including difficulties as adults)

Ways the negative effects can be reduced

One way is easing short-term separation with a replacement attachment figure. After James Robertson's work demonstrated that young children in hospitals suffered maternal deprivation and showed protest, despair and detachment, James and Joyce Robertson chose to take action and to further study maternal deprivation. They fostered a child (Jane) whose mother was about to go into hospital and found the transition was better if the child visited them with parents beforehand, if she brought something familiar and if routine was kept the same during the stay.

Another way is providing more individual care and stimulation. Skodak and Skeels (1945) found that children in orphanages who were given more stimulation or where there were more staff per child improved in IQ more than those who did not have more stimulation.

More will be said on ways to overcome the negative effects of deprivation when daycare is discussed later in this content section.

Evaluation of Bowlby's ideas

Summary of the strengths and weaknesses of Bowlby's theory of attachment

Strengths	Weaknesses
• Bowlby drew on many studies and their findings • He drew on many different theoretical perspectives • He used or drew on many different research methods • His theory had clear practical application and was acted upon	• He used evidence from animals, such as Harlow's and Lorenz's work, and it might not be legitimate to generalise from animals to humans • Some of the studies whose findings he used were not well-documented or well-controlled studies • His own study of 44 juvenile thieves, for example, lacked a 'normal' control group

Ainsworth's strange situation test and studies of attachment

Mary Ainsworth used a structured observation with carefully planned controls and procedures to study caregiver–child interactions. She was looking at attachment types and maternal sensitivity and devised her own procedure to study such issues. She also looked at two cultures, and later studies used her procedure in other cultures to examine differences in attachment types between cultures.

The strange situation test

The test involves a room set up with toys and chairs so that a mother and child can enter and play — rather like a waiting room. Observers can watch unseen through a one-way mirror. The situation involves a mother and child in the room, then a stranger entering, the mother leaving and other similar entrances and exits by the mother and the stranger. The idea is to study two reunions that occur during the procedure — when the child and mother are reunited as the mother comes into the room. One version of the test is shown in the table below.

A version of the strange situation, involving eight steps

1	The parent and baby enter the room, which is in a laboratory but set up with toys and chairs to be comfortable for the participants.
2	The parent does not interact with the baby, who is left to explore.
3	The stranger goes into the room, talks to the parent, then approaches the baby. At this stage the parent quietly leaves the room.
4	This is the first separation. The stranger tries to interact with the baby.
5	The parent comes in and comforts the baby, then leaves again. This is the first reunion followed by the second separation.
6	The stranger leaves the infant alone.
7	The stranger enters the room and begins to interact with the baby again. The parent is still out of the room. The second separation continues.
8	The parent comes in, greets and picks up the baby, while the stranger quietly leaves. This is the second reunion.

The mother is in control of the situation and can shorten the step or stop the procedure at any point.

Attachment types

From studies using the strange situation, Ainsworth identified three attachment types:

- **Securely attached** (Type B). In this type, the child is distressed when the mother leaves the room and seeks comfort from the mother when she returns. This is separation anxiety and is expected when a child has formed a secure attachment with the mother (or mother-figure). This type is linked to a responsive mother. In Ainsworth's (1978) study in Baltimore in the USA, about 70% of the infants were securely attached.
- **Anxious avoidant** (Type A; sometimes called anxious insecure). In this type, the child is not distressed when the mother leaves the room and tends to avoid her when she comes back. In Ainsworth's Baltimore study around 15% of the sample of 26 families had babies who were anxious avoidant.
- **Anxious resistant** (Type C; sometimes called ambivalent). In this type, the child stays close to the mother when the mother is in the room and becomes very distressed when she leaves. The child wants her for comfort when she comes back but then rejects her comforting. About 15% of babies in the Baltimore study belonged to this type.

Tip

Different books give different percentages for Ainsworth's work on attachment types but they all give a high percentage for Type B attachments and much lower percentages for the other two types. The different percentages arise because of different ways of classifying children into types. An allowance tends to be made for this in the exams.

Disorganised (Type D) is another attachment type, not one of Ainsworth's types but added by Main and Solomon in 1986. In this type, the child both approaches the mother on her return and avoids her.

Ainsworth and Bell (1969) looked at links between attachment type and type of mothering, and found that a less sensitive mother who did not respond to her infant's needs during feeding and who showed little face-to-face interaction did not have a securely attached child.

Evaluation of the strange situation procedure

Strengths

- The procedure is replicable and carefully itemised so that the situation is exactly the same for all mother–child pairs and observations can be compared. This gives reliability.
- The mother is in control with regard to the level of distress experienced by the child and can shorten the separation as much as she wants to, so ethical issues are covered at least to an extent.

Weaknesses

- The procedure could be said to be culture-specific, as the situation with a child sitting in a sort of waiting room and playing with toys alongside the mother and then the mother leaving occurs in the USA and other Western countries, but perhaps less so in other sorts of culture.
- There could be ethical criticisms as the child is deliberately made distressed. However, the mother knows exactly what the procedure is, so to an extent there is informed consent and right to withdraw — for the mother if not the child.

Comparing Uganda and Baltimore — two different cultures

Ainsworth studied mother–child interactions in Uganda as well, but carried out observations and interviews rather than using the strange situation test. She gathered information about the babies and also about the mothers' sensitivity. The Ugandan mothers tended to have securely attached babies who did not cry much and used their mother as a secure base from which to explore, and the Ugandan mothers were sensitive to their babies' needs.

Around 70% of the US mothers were sensitive mothers and had securely attached children as well, so there are similarities between the two cultures. The Ugandan mothers also had some Type A insecurely attached children as did the US mothers. The US study in Baltimore used the strange situation test but also interviews and observations at the child's home to obtain information about sensitive mothering. In the main it was reported that the two studies gave similar data, so the attachment types were thought to be universal.

Other cross-cultural studies looking at attachment types and child-rearing styles

- Grossman et al. (1985) in Germany used the strange situation and found more avoidant attachment types than in the US study.
- Sagi et al. (1985) in Israel found more ambivalent types than in the US study.
- Miyake et al. (1985) in Japan also found more ambivalent types than in the US study.
- Jin Mi Kyoung (2005) compared 113 US families and 87 Korean families and used the strange situation test too. There were a greater number of securely attached infants than of any other type, which reinforces the idea that attachment types are found in similar proportions in all cultures. However, there were some differences: for example, the Korean children stayed less close to their mothers than the US sample and explored more. Korean mothers were also more likely to get down on the floor and play with their infants straightaway.

Evaluating the cross-cultural studies

- Perhaps the higher proportion of avoidant children in Germany was caused by a lack of responsiveness on the part of the mothers, as Ainsworth might have said. However, perhaps it was because German mothers value and encourage independence more. From the strange situation findings it is hard to draw cause-and-effect conclusions.

- In Japan and Israel there might be fewer interactions with strangers and this might account for the different reactions. Perhaps the strange situation is testing cultural differences in child-rearing style rather than differences in responsive mothering.
- However, the same types emerged and the type most commonly found was the securely attached child. There seem to be universal types, as was first thought, even though there are some differences in proportions because of cultural differences.

Strengths

- The same procedure was used in the different countries, which should give reliable findings.
- There were three types observed in the different studies and this shows consistency.
- The main attachment type in nearly all studies is 'securely attached', which gives reliability to the method, as it is what would be expected given other research about sensitive mothering leading to secure attachment.

Weaknesses

- The task itself may have led to findings of cross-cultural differences rather than the sensitivity of the mothering.
- Cultures differ in many aspects, such as family structures, parenting styles, expectations and how children are viewed. The strange situation test does not take into account these differences.

Evaluation of Ainsworth's ideas about attachment

Summary of the strengths and weaknesses of Ainsworth's theory about attachment

Strengths	Weaknesses
• There is a great deal of evidence, including the work of Bowlby and Harlow	• The strange situation is laboratory-based and artificial, so it lacks validity
• The strange situation is laboratory-based and replicable, so it is reliable	• A fourth attachment type was later added, suggesting her theory was insufficient
• Ainsworth also used naturalistic observations that were valid	• Attachment and responsiveness are hard to measure, so hard to study reliably

Research into privation

Two central studies that look at privation are described and evaluated here. One of them is Curtiss's case study of Genie, mentioned earlier: this is the main study in detail for this application so is covered in depth here (instead of in the 'Studies in detail' section later on).

Privation (a key term) refers to an infant's lack of an attachment (a warm continuous relationship with a caregiver). This is different from deprivation, which occurs when an attachment is broken through separation. Children who are privated could have had an attachment figure at one time, if some extreme trauma and separation from such a figure have taken place. Usually privation is thought of as never having had an attachment figure.

There are documented cases of feral (wild) children — children who have not really been brought up by anyone and so are not socialised and do not understand social norms or show typical behaviour.

Koluchová's study: the Czech twins

- Koluchová (1972) studied a pair of twins in Czechoslovakia, as it was then. She documented their case and also returned to it later. She used the case study method and a lot of data were gathered.
- The twins were brought up in an institution for a year and then by an aunt for 6 months, so for the first 18 months they had a reasonably normal upbringing. Then their father remarried and they returned to the home.
- Their stepmother mistreated them badly, locked them in a room and beat them. This continued for over 5 years.
- They were considered to have been privated rather than deprived of an attachment figure. This was because, even though there might have been some attachment in their very early life, it was in an institution and only for a short time, and also because of the extremely bad conditions they experienced after 18 months.
- When found at the age of 7, they had bone disease and were small for their age. They could not talk or recognise pictures and were not able to undergo an IQ test. They were frightened of other people and their stage of development was about that of a 3-year-old.
- The boys went through various schools, starting in a school for children with severe learning difficulties. They were adopted by a woman who gave them special attention and over time they began to catch up and went to a normal school. At 11 their speech was normal for their age and at 15 their IQ was normal for their age.
- Both did well at school and went on to train in electronics.
- Koluchová documented in 1991 that both were married with children; they were happy and stable, and had warm relationships with their families.
- The conclusion of the case study is that the effects of privation are reversible.

Evaluation of the Czech twins study
Strengths
- It is known that the twins' development at the start was normal so that any problems came not from their nature but from their nurture. This gave a baseline measure at the start of the study.
- This was an in-depth case study where a lot of data were gathered and measures such as IQ tests were used, so it is likely that the data are valid and about the real-life situation of the twins.

- The study was longitudinal and so there are data about the reversibility of privation in the early years — it is hard to find evidence in this area so this case study is very useful.

Weaknesses
- The boys had each other and could have formed attachments with each other, which might have been enough.
- They would have formed an attachment to their aunt and perhaps in the institution, so perhaps were deprived of attachment rather than privated.
- It appears that the boys as adults are now happy and well adjusted, but it is hard to know what life is really like for them. They may be hiding certain feelings and emotions — there is no reason to assume that they are, but we cannot be sure.

Curtiss's study of Genie

Curtiss in 1977 wrote up a case study of a girl who was called 'Genie' by psychologists because she appeared as if from nowhere. This section describes and evaluates the 'Genie' study in some detail because it is the main study in detail for this application.

Aims

- to look at the progress or lack of progress of Genie after she was found at the age of 13, in order to find out more about development, particularly language development
- to help Genie towards normal development or at least to improve her quality of life

Case background

Genie (not her real name) was found at the age of about 13 years. She had been strapped to a 'potty chair' and mostly ignored in her room for all those years. She had only a few cotton reels to play with and her food was just left for her. She was not known about by the authorities for a long time but eventually came to light.

Genie's mother was afraid of Genie's father, who did not want Genie. The family first had one daughter who was sickly and cried a lot and who died at the age of 2 and then they had a son who had developmental problems. Grandparents took the son and brought him up for a little while and then he returned to his parents. Then Genie was born — she seemed normal at a 5-month check-up although she had a hip dislocation. She was seen by health service personnel at that stage. By 14 months Genie had not been paid much attention and her father did not like her, but when she was ill at that time she was seen by a paediatrician, who thought there might be some retardation. Genie's father seems to have used that as an excuse to shut her away and from then on Genie was isolated completely and tied to the potty chair. The family moved and isolated themselves. Genie's mother began to go blind and found it hard to go to speak to her as the father wanted her ignored. Her brother imitated his father and did not speak to her either.

In this way Genie spent the time until she was about 13 without being socialised or spoken to. Her father had thought she would not live after the age of about 12 and promised her mother she could get help after that, but he did not keep his promise. Genie's mother went to get help anyway and Genie was discovered. Genie's parents were charged with child abuse but her father killed himself on the day of the trial.

Case description

Data were gathered by working with Genie and observing her. There were also tests of language development, to see what she understood and what she could do. Videotapes and recordings were made and doctors were interviewed about Genie. She progressed and slowly began to be socialised, with regard to eating and communicating, for example. She learned to understand words and to identify objects. She understood numbers and started asking for the names of things around her. However, she never learned to use language normally — at least up until the time the funding ran out and the study was stopped. She did not walk normally either. After the study finished Genie went to live in an institution, where it is thought she still remains, her identity being protected for ethical reasons.

Case analysis

Genie was used as an experiment really — because there was interest in the possibility of a critical period for language development and Genie was found when she had passed that stage. On the face of it, she provided evidence for the existence of a critical period because she did not learn language normally — though she did learn some language and became able to communicate. However, she had had some interactions with others, at least early in her life, and may have heard some language before the start of the study. Another issue is that she may have had learning difficulties from the start. At 5 months she was said to be normal but a paediatrician thought she might be retarded when seen at 14 months.

Evaluation of the study of Genie

Strengths
- The case study is rich, detailed and thorough, with data including recordings and documented evidence, so there is validity. There are both quantitative and qualitative data that can be checked from more than one source, again emphasising validity.
- With regard to ethics, a strength is that her identity was protected at the time, giving privacy and confidentiality — though her picture is very well known and some claim that she has been identified.

Weaknesses
- Genie might not have developed normally in any case, and there is no 'before' data as a baseline measure to see how privation affected her.
- Ethically there were problems with the study. The psychologists and professionals fell out over the treatment of Genie because care for her and study of her were intermingled — many felt that she should have been treated rather than studied.

> **Tip**
>
> In this unit guide, two pieces of research focused on privation are described and evaluated in reasonable detail. This will be enough for many of the exam questions, but it would be better to revise at least one further study, so that you can offer more evidence on whether the effects of privation are reversible.

Are the effects of privation reversible?

This section uses the study of Genie and that of the Czech twins to discuss whether the effects of privation are reversible. Some further evidence is then briefly presented.

The study of Genie

- The study of Genie suggests that privation is not reversible.
- She was not able to properly develop language and, even after some time and given treatment, it was still clear that Genie was not developing in a typical way.
- However, there was some progress, as she did learn some language, how to communicate and how to interact with people — so to this extent at least the effects of privation may be reversible.
- One main problem with the study is the lack of a baseline measure: it was not completely clear that Genie was developing typically before being mistreated so badly, therefore the outcome may involve nature not nurture.

The study of the Czech twins

- The Czech twins study suggests that privation is reversible.
- They were developmentally behind for their age when found but they improved reasonably quickly.
- By the age of 11 their speech was normal for their age and by the age of 15 their IQ was normal for their age.
- They were given special care, so it might be that privation is only reversible with extra special care.
- On the other hand, Genie was given special care too, which suggests that this is not enough.
- A strength of the Czech twin study is that it was longitudinal and the twins were interviewed again many years later (1991) and found to be happy and settled as well as in stable relationships, so the evidence for privation being reversible is strong.
- However, they did have each other so their attachment to each other could have been enough, which would mean that this was not privation as such.

Other evidence

- Harlow's monkeys — the ones privated at birth, discussed earlier (page 52) — did not make good mothers themselves and found relationships difficult, which is evidence that the effects are not reversible.
- Freud and Dann (1951) studied a group of very young children who were liberated from the ghetto of Terezin and had been privated in that they were looked after by any adult who 'passed through' the camp. The children went to Britain and

developed normal intelligence in the main. This would suggest the effects of privation are reversible. However, the children were strongly attached to one another so, as in the case of the Czech twins, perhaps they were not completely privated.

Daycare and its effects on children

Daycare involves some separation from the mother or main caregiver, so findings about daycare can be used to discuss short-term separation. There are studies that show that daycare is beneficial for a child and studies that suggest that it is not. This section presents one study that is 'for' daycare and one that is 'against'. There are other studies that can be used.

Defining daycare

Daycare (a key term) refers to any situation where a child is cared for by someone other than parents for some or all of the day. Types of daycare include a crèche, which is very short-term separation, or full-time daycare, which is longer separation. Daycare includes care at day nurseries, by childminders or by relatives, and there are other forms such as playgroups.

Rules for daycare

There are rules regarding daycare and government officials who inspect daycare facilities. Daycare providers have to have plans for each child to ensure that they receive certain types of care, such as going outside regularly and being stimulated. There have to be sufficient staff for the number of children, and toilet and washing facilities have to be suitable. These rules are in place now and it can be claimed that they came from psychological studies into daycare that show what provision is suitable.

Research into daycare

Belsky and Rovine (1988) is one study suggested for this course but not explained in this unit guide. Jay Belsky has done a lot of work looking into daycare and the findings have affected government policy. For example, there is a general finding that children under the age of 1 year, if in daycare for more than 20 hours a week, do not benefit. In this section the two studies chosen are longitudinal ones, one done in the USA and one in the UK.

The NICHD study in the USA

The NICHD (National Institute of Child Health and Human Development) study followed children from birth and is a longitudinal study.

Aim

- to look at the effect of childcare on children

Procedure

Using a longitudinal design, the researchers gathered data by means of observation, interview and survey. There were 1,200 children involved and data were gathered from their birth to when they started school.

Results/conclusions

- Children who spent early continuous and intensive time in daycare were likely to have more behavioural problems later, such as aggressiveness or disobedience. Therefore the length of time in daycare is important. The behaviour was rated by parents and teachers.
- Nursery-type care (as opposed to care in the home) led to improvements in cognitive and language development but increased behavioural problems such as aggression or disobedience.
- Low-quality care was bad for children whose mothers lacked sensitivity. Good-quality care included responsive staff, attentive staff and a stimulating environment.
- In general it could be said that this study is against daycare, at least if it is for a long time each week and is low-quality care.

Evaluation of the NICHD study

Strengths

- This was a longitudinal study, therefore coverage was thorough, using the same children over time so individual differences could be taken into account.
- There was more than one research method, therefore validity could be checked, as could reliability.

Weaknesses

- There are many variables involved when studying childcare and it is very hard to draw meaningful conclusions. Development includes social, emotional and intellectual development so there are many aspects to consider, and also there are many factors affecting the child, including family background factors.
- The study is done in the USA and generalising to other cultures might not be appropriate. Cross-cultural studies, such as those done using the strange situation test (pages 56–57), suggest that child-rearing practices differ between cultures.

The EPPE project in the UK

The EPPE project ran from 1997 to 2003 and was funded by the UK government. This was a longitudinal study. The researchers followed children from the age of 3 or 4 and there was a special project for preschool children.

Aims

- to look at the impact of preschool provision on a child's intellectual and social/behavioural development
- to find out if social inequalities could be reduced by attendance at a preschool setting

Procedure

The study involved 3,000 children and methods included observations and interviews. There was a range of social backgrounds in the sample. Two groups were focused on, those in some sort of daycare centre and those who stayed at home. The 'home' children were a control group and 144 centres took part.

Results/conclusions

- High-quality care improved social, intellectual and behavioural development.
- The earlier a child started daycare, the greater the intellectual improvement.
- Children had better sociability, independence and concentration the longer they had been in daycare.
- Full-time attendance did not give higher gains than part-time attendance.
- Disadvantaged children were better off in good-quality daycare and in groups with mixed social background.
- The EPPE project is 'for' daycare at least if it is of good quality and has a mix with regard to social background.

Evaluation of the EPPE study

Strengths

- The control group and planned sample to include differences in social background meant that conclusions could be drawn more safely as there was a baseline measure of typical development without daycare.
- The longitudinal design meant individual differences were controlled for and taken into account and also a great deal of data could be gathered and compared.

Weaknesses

- The study had government funding and the government would benefit from having mothers at work and so from having children in daycare. If daycare helps children to develop in terms of intellect and behaviour, then that helps the government as well. So it could be claimed that the findings — in favour of daycare — were what the government would want. However, the researchers are well respected and there is no evidence for this criticism.
- Cross-cultural studies such as those looking at attachment types and child rearing (pages 56–57) tend to suggest cultural differences, so generalising from the UK to other cultures might not be appropriate.

Belsky's findings

Belsky considered the findings of both the NICHD and the EPPE projects and suggested that children should not spend too long in daycare. He concluded in 2006 that good-quality childcare, including that in daycare centres, can lead to better cognitive and language development. However, more time spent in daycare, especially more time in centre-based care, tended to lead to more problem behaviour. The important issues are quality, quantity and type of daycare.

Autism

This section looks at autism. First autism is defined, then two explanations for autism are considered and finally there is a discussion of how autism might affect a child's development.

> **Tip**
>
> You may have studied another developmental disorder in your course and if so you might prefer to revise that rather than learn about a different disorder.

content guidance

Defining autism

- **Autism** is part of the autistic spectrum disorder (ASD), which also covers the more common Asperger's Syndrome. Asperger's Syndrome is mild autism and usually discussions of autism focus on more severely autistic people.
- Autism affects more boys than girls and the ratio for more severe autism is four boys to every one girl.
- It is thought that about two people in every thousand (0.2%) have autism in this country.
- Groups of characteristics are used to diagnose autism rather than a specific set of characteristics, but in general people suffering from autism find it hard to read someone's emotions and tend to have communication problems. One main characteristic is that they have trouble forming relationships.
- Those with autism tend to be good at systems. About 10% of them have a special ability, often to do with systems such as maths, art or piano playing, and are called autistic savants.
- Another main characteristic is repeating a behaviour over and over again without getting bored. Often the behaviour involves sorting or systems.

Two explanations for autism

The two explanations covered in this unit guide are the theory of mind explanation (a cognitive explanation) and the extreme male brain explanation (a biological one). Both theories are linked to Baron-Cohen.

Theory of mind and autism

- Theory of mind refers to the ability to understand that other people's thoughts and understanding of the world are different from one's own, and is seen in children from around the age of 3.
- For example, when a child watches one doll 'hide' a marble from another doll while the other doll is absent, a child with theory of mind will understand that, though the child knows where the marble is, the other doll does not 'know'.
- There is evidence that children with autism do not have theory of mind.
- Baron-Cohen and Frith (1985) carried out a study of children with autism, children with Down's syndrome and typically developing children. Both the typically developing children and those with Down's syndrome had developed theory of mind but the children with autism had not. In the 'doll' experiment, autistic children, knowing that the marble had moved, thought that everyone else (including the doll) knew too — so when asked where the doll would 'look' for the marble, an autistic child would say that the doll would look where the child knows the doll is.
- The idea that autistic children do not have theory of mind is a cognitive explanation.
- Children with autism are high systematisers and low empathisers, which also fits with a cognitive explanation. If someone does not empathise with another, perhaps that goes with not being able to take another person's point of view, which is what theory of mind involves.

Extreme male brain and autism

- The idea that those with autism are low empathisers and high systematisers suggests a link to male brain features.
- It has been suggested that in autistic people, those male brain features are there to a greater extent than typical.
- Males are said to be better at visuo-spatial tasks such as map reading and jigsaws, which involve systems.
- Females are better at empathising and using both halves of the brain, as well as being better at language (in general — these are just *general* statements).
- The brains of boys grow more quickly than girls' brains and those with autism show greater growth in the brain.
- Females are better at working out body language than males, which goes with females being better at empathising.
- Putting the above evidence together, it can be seen why autism is said to be about having an extreme male brain.
- Females can have male brains — this is not about being a boy or a girl but about features of the brain. So this explanation does not conflict with the existence of females with autism.

How autism might affect a child's development

- Someone with autism has trouble making friends. This is because they find it hard to see another's point of view (lack of theory of mind) and also because of difficulties with empathising.
- Parents tend to arrange for friends to visit because friendships are important. They can help to prevent bullying, which can be a problem; and they can help the child with autism to develop social skills, at least to an extent.
- Children with autism differ. Some have special talents; some are very good at language, while others have great difficulty. So autism tends to affect different children differently.
- Bauminger and Kasari (2000) found that autistic children had fewer friendships and were more lonely but they understood loneliness less.
- Autistic children tend to have problems with communication, including learning language.
- Some autistic children can use language and it might seem that they are fluent, but often the understanding behind the words is lacking.
- There are sometimes difficulties with eye contact and non-verbal communication and these can link to problems with friendships, as friendships can rest on such social interactions.

Studies in detail

The main study that you need to know in detail for child psychology is Curtiss's (1977) study of Genie, which was explained in the content section for this application (pages

59–60). You need one other study from Bowlby (1944), Belsky and Rovine (1988) and Rutter and the ERA team (1998). Bowlby (1944), the 44 Juvenile Thieves study, was explained in detail on pages 49–51.

Evidence in practice: key issue and practical

Key issue

The key issue chosen in this unit guide is the issue of daycare and its effects on a child during development. Other issues (such as to what extent autism has a biological basis) could also be chosen and the material from the content section used.

Daycare and its effects on child development

Daycare is defined in an earlier section (page 62) — it refers to any care of a child that is not given by parents for some or all of the day. Examples are nurseries, childminding and care by relatives. Very young children can be in a day nursery from early in the morning to late at night 5 days a week, and some people think that is not good for the child. This links to the idea that parents and babies form attachments, and being without a special person who knows their needs can be very upsetting for a baby. On the other hand, it is said that parents who work and are fulfilled are perhaps happier and better parents, so daycare is a good thing.

The debate concerns whether daycare is good for the child (happier parents, a lot of stimulation, and learning to be sociable) or bad for the child (missing their main caregiver and the person that understands their needs best). It may not be that daycare is good or bad but that too much is bad or a certain type is bad (or good). This is what the debate is about and it is a key issue for society. This is because society needs workers and so working mothers are useful, but it also needs well-functioning adults so early upbringing is very important.

Explaining issues about daycare

In the content section, two studies were explained: one that showed that daycare in the main was good for a child's social, emotional and intellectual development (the EPPE study) and one that suggested that daycare could be detrimental in terms of aggressive behaviour (the NICHD study). Use those studies to present a balanced argument about the pros and cons of daycare. A summary might be as follows. High-quality daycare can be useful in terms of developing sociability and intellect. However, low-quality daycare is not useful and regulations are in place to ensure a good ratio of staff to children, good-quality stimulation and appropriate care. A key worker takes responsibility for an individual child, for example. These regulations have come about largely because of studies into daycare to ensure that if a child receives daycare it is beneficial for them.

Practical

You need to revise your own practical because you will have to answer questions based on what you did. The practical suggested here is one looking at attitudes to daycare and you will find this practical explained more fully in the 'Getting Started' booklet that goes with the course. The Edexcel website provides access to the specification, specimen assessment materials and the 'Getting Started' booklet.

Content analysis to look at attitudes to daycare

A content analysis was carried out using two newspapers to look at any mention of daycare or related topics concerning child rearing. Each mention was recorded and noted. Then the list was gone through to find categories, and reduced again to find underpinning ideas. In this way qualitative data were gathered and then listed into categories. It was found that there were themes about how children are viewed, the place of punishment and rewards in child rearing, and other issues. Mention was made of the quality of daycare provision and in general the findings support those of psychology — that rewards are better than punishments and that good-quality daycare is desirable rather than low-quality care.

Questions
&
Answers

This part of the guide presents questions for each of the two applications, first for Criminological Psychology and then for Child Psychology. For each application, the questions are divided into five sections, one for each area of the specification:

- Definition of the application
- Methodology/how science works
- Content
- Studies in detail
- Evidence in practice: key issue and practical

Choose one area of the specification and revise the material using this unit guide. Work through the questions for your chosen area, answering them yourself without reading the advice on how to answer the question and without reading the answers given. Then mark your own answers, and read through the advice on what is required. Did you interpret the question successfully? Read through the answers given and note where the marks are awarded. Finally, read through the examiner's comments to see what a full answer should include.

Examiner's comments

All questions and answers are followed by examiner's comments. These are preceded by the icon e. The comments on the questions indicate what is required in the way of an answer, and show areas that need focus, for instance where there are two instructions (e.g. describe and evaluate) or where the focus is specific (e.g. on validity of a method). The comments on the answers indicate where credit is due and point out areas for improvement, specific problems and common errors such as poor time management, lack of clarity, weak or non-existent development, irrelevance, misinterpretation of the question and mistaken meanings of terms.

Criminological psychology

Definition of the application

(a) Define what is meant by 'token economy'. (2 marks)

(b) Imagine that you had to explain to a friend what criminological psychology is about. Outline two areas that are covered. (4 marks)

(a) For this question make sure you give enough for the 2 marks. If in doubt, give an example to show understanding.

(b) There are 4 marks here, so assume 2 for each area. You need a clear outline of each. An example helps to show understanding.

■ ■ ■

Answers

(a) Token economy refers to a treatment that is used with regard to criminal or abnormal behaviour — any behaviour that society wishes to improve or eliminate. The treatment is based on operant conditioning principles where rewards are given for good behaviour in the form of tokens to spend on what the individual wants. ✓ This is positive reinforcement. Maladaptive behaviour is thus replaced with desired behaviour. ✓

This answer would get the 2 marks as it clearly shows understanding.

(b) Criminological psychology covers crime and antisocial behaviour and what might cause them, for example labelling or learning by observing others. Social learning theory says that we imitate role models ✓ and if someone's role model shows criminal behaviour then they are likely to copy it and become a criminal as well. ✓ The area also covers eyewitness memory and how it is unreliable. For example, if you ask someone about the speed of a car when it hit another car compared to asking someone else about the speed of a car when it smashed another car, the first estimate is likely to be lower than the second because 'smashed' suggests a faster speed. ✓ This suggests that eyewitness testimony is unreliable and if in a court a witness is asked a leading question such as 'Did you see the broken glass?', they are likely to 'recall' broken glass. ✓

This answer gets all 4 marks because both the areas (social learning and eyewitness testimony) are clearly explained. Note that in this answer the identification of the two areas has not been awarded marks, as identification marks tend not to be given at A2. They may sometimes be given, but it is best to work on the principle that they will not be and to learn more than you need.

Question 2

Methodology/how science works

(a) Outline one difference between field and laboratory experiments. (3 marks)

(b) Evaluate field experiments in terms of their ethics. (3 marks)

(a) Note that here one difference is wanted but there are 3 marks. You are likely to need examples to illustrate the difference you choose, as otherwise you might not provide enough for the marks.

(b) There are 3 marks available and all the points must be about ethics. It is useful to give at least one way in which field experiments are ethical and at least one way in which they are not, as this will help to give the required depth.

■ ■ ■

Answers

(a) The main difference between field and laboratory experiments is that field experiments take place in the field and in a natural setting whereas laboratory experiments take place in a controlled and artificial setting. ✓ For example, Yarmey (2004) did field experiments by asking people on the streets one by one what they recalled about someone who had just asked them a question (for example), so the study was in the participants' natural setting in their everyday lives. However, Loftus and Palmer (1974) asked questions of groups of students in a controlled and artificial environment where they watched films of car accidents. ✓ So Yarmey's work tends to be seen as more valid, being more about real-life behaviour, and Loftus's work tends to be seen as less valid, as the setting is controlled and artificial. ✓

There are 3 marks here but note that a lot needs to be said to explain the difference. You may be tempted in these short-answer questions to write an answer quickly and move on, but it is useful to give a little more material to be sure of the marks.

(b) Field experiments are ethical in that they do not ask people to perform in a controlled and artificial setting; the participants are in their own environment so might be less distressed than in a laboratory experiment. ✓ A problem is that people are often not asked whether they will take part when in a field experiment because surprise is an important element of getting valid and reliable results. So informed consent is often not obtained, though participants can be asked at the end whether they are happy for their results to be included. ✓ This is part of the debrief. They can also be assured of confidentiality and privacy, other ethical guidelines that must be adhered to according to the British Psychological Society. ✓

This answer gives enough for the 3 marks. Four ethical issues are mentioned (distress, informed consent, right to withdraw and debrief). All are well related to the field experiment as a method, which is important. Do not talk about ethical issues in general.

Question 3

Content

(a) Compare two explanations for criminal/antisocial behaviour. (6 marks)

(b) Describe and evaluate two studies of eyewitness testimony. (12 marks)

(c) Describe and evaluate two ways of treating offenders. (12 marks)

(a) There are 6 marks here for comparing the two explanations that you have studied. Comparison involves giving similarities and differences. It is helpful to use expressions such as 'however' and 'in contrast' to make it clear that you are comparing.

(b) This is an essay question. You should choose two studies of eyewitness testimony and look at them in depth. Essays are marked using levels of quality, such as a higher level of mark if more than one study is addressed (up to around half the marks only if only one study is addressed, for this question) and a high level if terms are used appropriately. From about halfway up the marks, a level will start to ask for evaluation too, not just description. Aim to balance your answer with half on each study and half again on description and evaluation.

(c) This is another essay question. It is straightforward in asking you to both describe and evaluate, and (as with the previous question) you are asked to cover two areas of content. Divide the question into halves for the two ways and into halves again for describing and evaluating. Remember to use appropriate terminology and to write in clear sentences so as to make your points effectively.

■ ■ ■

Answers

(a) Social learning theory can explain antisocial and criminal behaviour. It suggests that we copy role models so observing antisocial behaviour, for example, would lead to it being imitated. The self-fulfilling prophecy also explains such behaviour because if someone is labelled then they tend to live up to the label and display appropriate behaviour. Both these explanations involve the effect of others on behaviour, ✓ so both are 'social' in showing that social norms and customs can get passed on because other people either demonstrate them or label people. ✓

The theories are different because one is a theory of how we learn in all situations whereas the other is in specific situations where a label is given, which is not likely to be all situations. ✓ Another difference is that social learning theory is usually seen as a learning theory whereas the self-fulfilling prophecy is a theory from the social approach. ✓ Both the theories focus on environmental influences and not on biological ones, so both are about nurture and not nature. ✓ The social learning theory comes from the learning theory idea that people are born as a blank slate and that experiences make people what they are, and the theory of the self-fulfilling prophecy also suggests that it is experience that affects what someone becomes and not inherited characteristics. ✓

🖉 There is enough detail here for the 6 marks as the points are clear and there is some elaboration. It is not easy to find enough comparison points to get 6 marks. It is useful to think of some general themes such as the approach to which the explanation belongs, or ideas about science or nature–nurture that are shared or different between the explanations.

(b) Studies of eyewitness testimony are important as they point mainly to potential problems. If a defendant is prosecuted and the only evidence rests on eyewitness testimony, studies have shown that there is a serious risk of a miscarriage of justice. Loftus has done many studies in this area and most point to problems with eyewitness and victim memory. For example, Loftus and Palmer (1974) found that if questions used different verbs to indicate speed of a car, such as 'hit', 'smashed', 'collided' or 'bumped', then participants gave a different estimate of speed in their answers. They gave a higher estimate of speed if the word was 'smashed' than if the word was 'collided'. The conclusion was that even one word in a question turned it into a leading question, and the word guided judgement, in this case of speed. Another study asked about a 'barn' that was not present in a scene, and yet a number of participants still 'recalled' the barn. Leading questions seem to change the memory and this shows that care must be taken when questioning witnesses such as eyewitnesses.

Yuille and Cutshall (1986) did a different sort of study, not an experiment, whereas most research into the unreliability of eyewitness testimony uses experiments. Yuille and Cutshall found a case where about 21 eyewitnesses had given evidence about a murder they saw in the street. The researchers went back to the witnesses (only about 13 of them, as the others did not take part) and asked them again about the whole incident. They found that the witnesses remembered a lot about what had happened, including more detail than was found in their statements taken by the police at the time. So the field study showed that eyewitness testimony is reliable (the same findings were found when the witnesses were asked again) whereas Loftus's laboratory experiment found the opposite.

The studies themselves are not without criticism though. They tend to be mainly laboratory-based and as such they do not involve any emotion that an eyewitness might be expected to feel. Even studies looking at emotional issues tend to be controlled (for example, those that find that there is a weapon effect, i.e. when a weapon is present, an eyewitness is likely to focus on that rather than on other factors in a scene). Even if the experiment is a field experiment, controls still tend to mean that the situation is not natural, so validity can be questioned. But Yuille and Cutshall asked real witnesses about a real murder so there was validity in that sense.

🖉 This answer is well expressed, uses psychological terms and presents two studies as asked. The answer considers the Loftus and Palmer study about estimating speed, the

Loftus study about a 'barn' being present, the Yuille and Cutshall study and the study on weapon effect, though the two more detailed studies would be the ones marked. If you do more than is asked, then the marker will mark all and credit the best. There is credit for the introductory comments that studies are important as they show we must question eyewitness testimony so that defendants have a fair trial. AO2 credit is given for the comment that laboratory studies exclude emotions that would normally be present and for the comment about controls making studies unnatural. More AO2 credit could have been earned by adding that Loftus herself points out that it tends to be peripheral information that misleads people, rather than central evidence, and studies often focus on peripheral information (such as the 'barn'). This answer is likely to be in the top band (10 to 12 marks).

(c) Cognitive–behavioural techniques such as anger control programmes are aimed at those who can learn to access their thoughts and to control those that lead to anger and aggression. Anger management programmes can include self-instructional training and role play. Social skills training can help interactions with others. This can reduce frustration and anger that might lead to aggressive behaviour.

Token economy programmes use principles of operant conditioning. The idea is that appropriate (such as non-aggressive) behaviour should be rewarded, and inappropriate (aggressive) behaviour should either be punished or there should be negative reinforcement. Tokens are given for appropriate behaviour after those giving the therapy have set out what this is; these are positive reinforcers. These tokens can then be exchanged for something desired, such as more television watching, a visit, or time doing exercise.

These programmes do have problems. The token economy programme may work in the institution itself, although it may be difficult as there are other ways in which those in institutions are rewarded, such as by other prisoners, and these may indeed reward aggression. A problem is that even if it does work in the institution, once the individuals have left, the pattern of reinforcements will stop, and people are likely to go back to their original situation, where aggression may have been rewarded within a peer group, for example.

Anger control programmes may have similar problems in that what has been learned may not be transferred out of the setting of the programme. In addition, individuals must be able to focus on their thoughts and this suggests that aggression comes from thoughts. If it arises from biological causes, cognitive–behavioural therapy is unlikely to be helpful. It is hard to evaluate treatment programmes that are in place for offenders as there are many factors to consider, including possibly the biological make-up of the offender as well as other influences on their behaviour such as social learning and their early environments.

This answer is reasonably thorough in that two treatments are outlined in some detail and both are evaluated, to an extent at least. The essay is well structured in that the description of both comes first, followed by the evaluation, so it is clear that both injunctions are being addressed. The description of anger management programmes is rather general and the evaluation of both is rather general. Some studies giving evidence for or against the success of the treatments would add depth and detail. This essay is likely to be in the top band of 10–12 marks.

Studies in detail

(a) Describe the procedure of Loftus and Palmer's (1974) study. (5 marks)

(b) Compare the research methods of Loftus and Palmer (1974) and one other study from Yuille and Cutshall (1986), Charlton et al. (2000) and Gesch et al. (2003). (6 marks)

(a) There are 5 marks here for the procedure alone, so you need a lot of detail.

(b) There are 6 marks here for comparing the two studies in terms of methodology. Comparing involves similarities and differences so focus on those. Points do not have to be in depth — just showing that different research methods or different designs are used can be enough. In any of these types of question where there is a choice, make sure you say clearly which study or studies you have chosen — this seems obvious, but is not always done.

■ ■ ■

Answers

(a) Loftus and Palmer (1974) got students to volunteer for their study and showed them films of car crashes. There were two parts to their study and in the first they changed the verb of a question they asked about the car crashes. ✓ They changed the verb so that they asked either about how the cars 'hit', 'smashed', 'collided', 'bumped' or 'contacted'. They used 45 students and broke them up into groups of 9 with each group having one of the verbs in the special question. ✓ The researchers administered a questionnaire and the crucial question was, 'How fast were the cars going when they ___?' The gap was filled with 'hit', 'smashed', 'collided', 'bumped' or 'contacted' ✓ and the replies (estimates of speed in miles per hour) were recorded. ✓ The second part of the study involved participants (students again) who had the word 'smashed' or the word 'hit', and the question in the second part of the study was whether there was broken glass. ✓

There are 5 marks here and you can see that you need a lot of detail to gain full marks for just the procedure. This means that for each part of a study, for the studies in detail at least, you need to make sure you know enough information.

(b) Loftus and Palmer (1974) used a laboratory experimental method and Yuille and Cutshall used a field study that they called a case study, so their research methods were very different. ✓ A lab experiment has careful controls and is replicable whereas a case study has few controls and is hard to replicate. (✓) In fact, though, Yuille and Cutshall were replicating a police investigation and using previously collected data, so someone else could have done the same and then asked the participants yet again, to check Yuille and Cutshall's results. ✓ The case study took place in the participants' own environment, which can help validity, but the lab experiments were in an unfamiliar setting up to a point. (✓) However, as students were used and they were in their own setting, there may have been some validity. ✓ The Yuille and Cutshall study used a real-life murder and real witnesses so there was some validity in the task, whereas Loftus and Palmer (1974) used films of car accidents and asked about the speed of the cars, which was not real life for the students — they may not have cared as they were not emotionally involved. ✓

🖉 This answer seems detailed but it has been given only 4 marks. It is possible that a mark could be given in each of the two places where there is a bracketed tick; however, make sure of the marks by giving more information. You could compare the participants and specify that one used students and one used real witnesses — this is said, but not as a separate point, so is worth stating again. You could also mention that the laboratory experiment may have been more ethical as it did not arouse real emotions, whereas in the Yuille and Cutshall study the victim did not want to take part and neither did some of the other witnesses — their study may have been more distressing because it was about a real murder.

Evidence in practice: key issue and practical

(a) Describe one key issue in criminological psychology. (4 marks)

(b) Explain how you carried out either a content analysis or an analysis of articles within criminological psychology. (4 marks)

(a) There are 4 marks here for describing the issue itself and not psychological findings about it.

(b) This question is about your practical, which would be either a content analysis or a summary and analysis of article sources. The 4 marks are for explaining how you carried out the analysis, not what was found.

■ ■ ■

Answers

(a) The issue of whether eyewitness testimony is reliable is a key issue in criminological psychology because people have been imprisoned on the strength of eyewitness testimony alone. ✓ This is not fair if the testimony is unreliable — society needs to be sure that convictions are fair and firm. It costs a lot of money to have another trial, the wrong person is punished and the real criminal is free, so there are many reasons for making sure that eyewitnesses give reliable testimony. ✓

This answer is clear and gets 2 marks — it is possible that it would get a third mark as an identification mark, but act on the principle that there is no identification mark. Two other marks could come from saying that in the USA some states have rules about how eyewitnesses are questioned because they want to be sure that witnesses are reliable, and there are rules about identification in line-ups in particular so that the wrong person is not identified. You could also give an example of someone who was imprisoned wrongly on the strength of eyewitness testimony alone.

(b) I found two articles on eyewitness testimony, one about someone convicted using witness memory and the other about police and court rules for obtaining eyewitness testimony. Both articles were on the internet and both were from the USA. I read each article and made notes on what was said. I then wrote up the notes briefly to form two summaries, one of each article. I actually wrote up two summaries as I had to summarise my first one to reduce it, as it was too long and I had really just made a list of points, which my teacher said was not a summary. Then I put the two summaries into a report and the final step was to use concepts I had learned about to explain the two summaries.

🖭 This answer would be marked using levels as it is about the practical, which is not marked on a point-by-point basis but depending on the quality of the answer. Here the explanation is about how the analysis was done, including how the articles were found, although just the information that they were on the internet is given — more detail about the search would be useful. The answer states what the articles were but not how they were found. Then there is more about how the practical was carried out as it is explained that the summarising was done twice, which is useful detail. A final point about adding some psychological information is given, again being about how the analysis was done, which is relevant. This answer is more likely to get 2 or 3 marks than 4, as it is quite brief and does not give very clear information on how the articles were found or why those particular ones were chosen.

Child psychology

Definition of the application

Explain the difference between deprivation and privation. (2 marks)

>  You need to define the two terms here and then say how they are different. This can be done in one sentence, but be sure to give enough information if you only write one sentence.

■ ■ ■

Answer

Deprivation refers to the situation when a child has formed an attachment with a caregiver that is a close bond (which, for example, includes elements such as stranger fear), and this attachment is broken for some reason. Privation occurs when a child has formed no attachment at all — or some extreme trauma has wiped out any previous short attachment. ✓ The difference is that in privation there is no attachment at all and in deprivation an attachment has been formed and has been broken. ✓

>  This answer gets both marks as it is clear and detailed. Aim for this sort of answer, which is likely to be more than is needed, to be sure of earning the marks. For a question requiring a definition of the terms, two ticks would be given where the first tick appears above, but because this question is about the difference the second tick is not given until the end.

Methodology/how science works

(a) Explain three features of a case study that make it a good choice of research method in child psychology. (6 marks)

(b) Explain why Ainsworth used the strange situation test. (4 marks)

(a) It is important to focus on case studies as used in child psychology, though the area is broad and could include Freud's style of case study. You have to learn the Genie case study, so you can use features from that but you should keep them general.

(b) This is a different sort of question from what might be expected — such as 'Describe what is meant by the strange situation test' — but be ready for such questions. It was thought more useful to give this sort of question here rather than more standard ones such as 'describe' and 'evaluate', but practise those as well. Here there are 4 marks, so one way to answer is to find four points and explain them clearly.

■ ■ ■

Answers

(a) One feature is the qualitative data that are gathered, which are useful because there is a lot of depth. ✓ For example, with a child like Genie, detail is needed, including in-depth background information as well as in-depth information about her abilities and development. ✓ Another common feature is the focus on one unique individual. This is good because you could say that each child is individual, with different attachment experiences, for example, and different environmental influences and social learning. ✓ So individual differences are covered, which means the study is more likely to be valid. ✓ Another feature is also about validity — that many different methods are used within the case study, such as psychological testing, observation, questionnaires and interviewing, and then triangulation can be used ✓ to see if data from the different methods agree, in which case the data are said to be both reliable and valid. ✓

Full marks are gained here because each feature is clear and a little more is given to show that the feature is understood. That would give 1 mark for each feature. Then in each case there is elaboration. It would be safer to include even more, as the marking here has assumed that a brief identification and outline of the feature are enough for a mark in each case — just a bit more than an identification mark — whereas a little more may be expected. Take no chances!

(b) Ainsworth used the strange situation as it used controls and she could then compare findings. She used the same set of steps for each mother-and-child pair so that she could make comparisons. ✓ She used the test to study attachments between mothers and babies, in particular stranger fear, so she devised a situation where a stranger was in the presence of the child alone so that the reaction could be studied. It is not easy to find such a situation without waiting for a long time so the set-up situation was useful. ✓ She used the test because she could compare between cultures — having a stranger enter and a mother leave is something that happens in all cultures so the test is replicable within and between cultures, which makes it useful. ✓ Additionally, she used the test because there could be more than one observer behind glass and so the findings could be tested for inter-observer reliability. It is hard to measure mother–child interactions scientifically and without interpretation so having more than one observer is useful. ✓

📝 Giving four reasons for 1 mark each is a successful strategy for this sort of question (though not the only strategy, as one reason elaborated upon with an example can gain more than 1 mark). Note the depth of each point.

Content

(a) Why is it of interest whether the effects of privation are reversible? (2 marks)

(b) What is meant by the evolutionary basis of attachment? (3 marks)

(c) Sadie is concerned because she needs to use daycare for her 1-year-old son but she wants to be sure that he is well looked after and developing well. She has read up on studies that show that daycare is a good thing, but she has also heard that daycare can be detrimental. Write out a report for Sadie giving pros and cons of using daycare and a summary of what to look for in good daycare. (12 marks)

(a) You might not have thought of a question like this but it is useful to practise using your information in different ways. There are 2 marks so make sure you give two clear points or give an example to elaborate.

(b) This is a definition question, but when there are 3 marks you need to give enough detail to earn them, such as examples.

(c) This is a different style of essay question to show that 'describe and evaluate' is not the only way to ask these questions. For this essay you need to give information on what is good and what is not so good with regard to daycare, and also a list of what makes daycare successful. You will have looked at one study that is 'for' daycare and one that is 'against', so you can use those in your answer.

■ ■ ■

Answers

(a) Privation is seen in children who have not had the chance to form attachments with anyone and so are not socialised in the usual sense. Most children have an attachment figure (or more than one) and form a close bond, which helps them to establish a safe and secure base. However, privated children do not have an attachment figure and their socialisation can cause problems for them. So it is of interest whether the effects of privation can be reversed so that early problems will not get in the way of later development. ✓ Privation has been shown to cause language problems and other problems with social norms and customs, as Curtiss's Genie study shows, and such difficulties can affect the individual and also cause difficulties for society. ✓

The marks here come later, though the definitions are useful to set the scene for the points made. These sorts of questions often need quite a bit of detail so that the points are clearly made.

(b) Evolution is about survival of the fittest, where any characteristic that helps an organism survive means it is more likely that that organism reproduces and passes on their genes. If that characteristic rests on genes then it is likely to

question

reappear and to survive as it leads to reproduction of those genes. The idea with regard to attachment is that it is a characteristic that leads to survival and later to reproduction and that it is carried through genes. ✓ Babies who formed attachments with their caregivers would be more likely to be cared for and develop normally — for example, signals such as crying would bring sensitive mothering and secure attachments. ✓ If those babies were more likely to survive then they would grow up and reproduce their genes. So genes giving attachment behaviour would survive. ✓

There are 3 marks here as the explanation is clear. First, evolution theory in general is explained, and then attachment is fitted into this theory, with some examples such as crying and sensitive mothering.

(c) The EPPE study in the UK showed that daycare was a good thing. It looked at children over the age of 3 years. The study found that children attending nursery were more sociable, for example, and their intellectual development and emotional development were good as well. They found that full-time nursery was not better than part-time, however, so there was little additional value in a child being in daycare full time.

The NICHD study in the USA suggested that daycare was not good, in that children in daycare were more likely to show aggression and have behavioural difficulties. This was for children who spent intensive time in daycare when they were young, so the length of time spent in daycare was seen to be important. If you just use daycare for your son two or three times a week there might not be such problems, and the EPPE study suggests that daycare will do your son good.

Note, however, that the EPPE study looked at children aged 3 and more, whereas your son is younger than that. Belsky showed that under the age of 1 year a child is likely not to benefit from daycare if it is for more than 20 hours a week. Your son is 1 year old so is in a position to benefit, hopefully, as long as he is not in daycare for too long over the week. Belsky's finding here reinforces the findings of the NICHD study. Daycare was found in the NICHD study to improve language development and cognitive development, even though there was more aggression, so the NICHD study found some benefits.

The main finding seems to be that the type of care and the length of daycare are important. The NICHD study showed that low-quality care was bad in particular for children whose mothers lacked sensitivity. You need to look for responsive and attentive staff and a stimulating environment. You need to look for a high staff–child ratio so that there are few children for each member of staff to look after, and you need to check that there is a policy of having a key worker for your son. These policies are in place in the UK in any case because of studies such as Belsky's and the NICHD study, as well as the EPPE study. Each nursery has an Ofsted report which you can look at, so you can find out about the performance of specific nurseries.

☑ This answer is quite comprehensive and uses the two studies well to focus on what Sadie needs to know and what she could do to ensure her son is well looked after. There is good use of terminology such as 'sensitivity', 'responsive' and 'cognitive development', and the writing is clear, so with regard to good and clear communication the top level in an essay marking scheme would be reached. The description of findings of studies is fairly detailed and there is some evaluation, for example noting that the EPPE study looked at children aged 3 and over whereas Sadie's son is 1 year old. The focus of the report is good, in that it ends by suggesting the sort of care to look out for. This answer should reach the top level of 10–12 marks.

Question 9

Studies in detail

(a) **Evaluate Bowlby's study of 44 Juvenile Thieves in terms of its methodology.**

(4 marks)

(b) **Explain three important results and/or conclusions of Curtiss's (1977) study of Genie.**

(3 marks)

(a) There are 4 marks here — this tends to be standard for evaluation questions, although some are given more marks. One way of answering is to give four clear evaluation points, all focused on method.

(b) There are 3 marks here and this suggests that each finding that you give should be clearly explained rather than simply identified. If there were identification marks you would expect 6 marks, 2 marks for each finding.

■ ■ ■

Answers

(a) Bowlby pointed out that his control group was also from the centre and so they were not typically developing children. He thought that a control group from a different setting and with typically developing children would be a better baseline measure. ✓ However, he did use many methods such as interviewing the parents and giving the children psychological testing. This means that validity is more likely as different methods obtained similar findings, which suggests the data are both reliable and valid. ✓

One issue was that the study was not replicable because the sample came from a centre where Bowlby worked as a psychiatrist, and as the children were also being treated they could not be used again because their situation and behaviour would not be the same. ✓ However, others could be tested in the same way to find out if those who had had maternal deprivation did turn out to be affectionless, so to that extent the study is replicable. ✓ Bowlby's study was ethical in that he was trying to find things out about juvenile delinquents who were also thieves to see if he could help them, so there was a practical reason for the study and the children who were participants were being supported and treated; also, their identities were kept secret and confidentiality was maintained. ✓

There are more than 4 marks here and the points are thoroughly made and well focused on the study. Points should all relate to the specific study and not be general. For example, it is not appropriate here to make the general point that a study in the field, such as Bowlby's, can be unethical because of lack of informed consent, because that was not the case with Bowlby's study.

(b) One result is that Genie developed some understanding of language and body language after she had been found, possibly as a result of imitating others or developing cognitively after being found. ✓ She could have copied the signs others made, which would show social learning theory at work, or she could have developed maturationally in the sense of developing understanding. However, another finding is that she did not develop typical language for her age, so she did not catch up after her severe privation. ✓ She could manage some language but not fluently, and the language she could use was very hard to understand. A third conclusion is a more general one — that it is hard to draw conclusions from the study because there is not enough information to show that there were not developmental issues in the first place, before her privation. She may have had learning difficulties which meant she would not have developed language fully in any case, for example, so the findings would be about nature and not nurture. ✓

🖉 The 3 marks are earned here as the three results/conclusions are very clearly outlined and there is elaboration.

Question 10

Evidence in practice: key issue and practical

(a) Outline the findings of the content analysis or article summaries that you carried out as your practical within child psychology. (4 marks)

(b) Evaluate the content analysis or article summaries that you carried out as your practical within child psychology. (4 marks)

(a) This is about the findings, which are results and/or conclusions, so do not explain how you found the material or what the methodology was. This is not about evaluation either.

(b) This is about evaluation of your practical, so do not describe the practical at all — just consider strengths and weaknesses.

■ ■ ■

Answers

(a) I found that daycare is thought of as being helpful, in particular for problem children whose behaviour needs to be controlled. I found that a newspaper carried more comments about daycare being better than bad parenting than comments about daycare being bad for a child because of separation from the attachment figure. I also found that nurseries were talked about most and there was little mention of childminding or other sorts of daycare.

This answer would be marked using levels because it is about your practical. There is not a lot of information here for the 4 marks; however, the answer is well focused and three findings are given. It is not that there is a mark for each finding; although there is good use of terms here (such as 'attachment figure'), the findings are rather general. Figures would be good if a content analysis was used, or more detail from articles if they were used. This would get 2 or 3 of the 4 marks.

(b) My content analysis only covered one newspaper on one day and in one country. There might be different comments on different days because current issues in politics might guide what is reported. Also there might be different comments in different newspapers because some are more 'pro' government and some are 'anti' government, and in the UK currently there is more likely to be praise for daycare because of a desire to get mothers back to work. Another point is that this was a content analysis in the UK, whereas a lot of studies are done in other countries, such as the USA and Sweden (e.g. NICHD in the USA and Andersson in Sweden). Also I did the analysis on my own so there might be subjectivity in my analysis of themes and counting of instances, whereas another person may have given the study inter-rater reliability.

e This answer would be marked using levels because it is about your practical. There is not a lot of information here for the 4 marks; however, the answer is well focused and quite a bit of detail in evaluation is given. There are points about different days, different newspapers, different cultures and subjectivity, as well as some good discussion of political influences on media. Giving the names of two studies to illustrate raises the level of the answer, and more of the same would add that final mark, as this answer is likely to get 3 marks and not quite the 4 available.